Two by
Two by Two

Dwight

These are plays
written because of
things heard from
people on the bridge.

Martin

Two by Two by Two

Three Comedies

Martin P. Kelly

Written to be performed
at The Bridge Theater
Whitehall, New York

Cover design by The Troy Book Makers

Royalty quotes and acting copies are available for productions both in professional and community theaters.
Call 518/461-5411

This book is published for:
Riverview Entertainment Productions, Inc.
E-Mail: markell2@localnet.com

ISBN: 978-1-61468-012-3

Previous plays published by Martin P. Kelly:

"A Marriage Of True Minds"
"Diplomat For All Times"
"Fall From Grace
"Champlain Onward"
"Cases On The Canal"
"Christmas On The Canal"

All of the above are contained in the anthology:
"Plays From The Bridge"

Special thanks to:

David Mohn
Managing Director
The Bridge Theater
Whitehall, NY

* * *

The estate of the late
Thomas S. Kelly

* * *

Susan Ingerson

* * *

J. William Hickman

Contents

"Free at Last"

A New Comedy

By Martin P. Kelly

Note from the Author

When many of my married friends who worked most of their lives decided to retire, each person in the marriage appeared to believe that the spouse would want to do the same things they wanted to do. Perhaps, one would want to start a business or consulting service at home while the spouse might want to work as a travel consultant or provide a service based on his or her previous occupation.

In many instances, these aspirations proved surprises for the spouses in these marriages. This comedy is built around what might happen in such a case.

MPK

"Free At Last"
ACT ONE

Scene 1

(At curtain rise, Cathy Michaels is on the phone in an enthusiastic conversation. The time is the present and the set is the modest living room of a retired couple. Matt, the husband, is a former teacher and Cathy a former Chamber of Commerce promotion assistant)

CATHY: That's right, Linda, they hired me this morning. I'm going to be responsible for all kinds of tours. Yes! This is one of the biggest travel agencies in the region, and the world. Of course! When I book a tour, I not only get a commission, I also get to go free and Matt is included in my freebie transportation and hotel. Think of it, all the cruises I ever wanted to take and places I wanted to visit when I retired. It's the chance of a lifetime! My experience working with the regional Chamber of Commerce gives me lists of potential groups and I'm on good terms with hundreds of them. And, you know I have no trouble talking on the phone, stranger or no!

Yes, Matt should love it. After he retired in June, he said he was through teaching kids and following rules that didn't do any good anyway.

I can't wait to tell him about my retirement plan. Oh! By the way, if you and Alex want to join one of our tours, I'll get you a good price. *(Laughs)* Talk to you soon!

(She hangs ups phone and exits into bedroom to change from her business clothes. A few moments later, Matt comes through front door, puts down brief case and goes to the phone. He dials.)

MATT: Hello, Harry! Hey, I just want to tell you I enjoyed meeting with you this morning and I think your idea is tremendous. It would really give the school district a shot in the arm and help support some of our...I mean your pet projects.

No, I didn't retire too soon. I just wanted to get away from the teaching schedule...you know, 7:30 in the morning with a classroom full of yawning kids who didn't eat much breakfast...their eyes still bleary from video games, computers and text messaging. Yeah! You know what I mean. We should have had a nurse at the door giving all of them caffeine shots every morning. Of course, when they do wake up, they're sneaking cell calls to each other during class or else text messaging one another. No, Harry! I'm looking forward to sitting in the backyard for a good deal of the rest of my life, reading what I want to read, listening to music that I want to listen to and dozing when not reading or listening. After 30 years of dealing with school kids, I'm ready for my escape to my own reality.

Thanks again Harry for lunch. Well, yes Harry, but you know my retirement plans! Okay, okay, I promise to think over your proposition.

(Hangs up phone as Cathy calls from other room..)

CATHY: Is that you, Matt!

MATT: Honey, if it's someone else, you're in trouble!

CATHY: *(Enters in more relaxed outfit)* You're all the trouble I want! *(Embraces him)* Now, sit down. Do I have news for you!!

MATT: Good! I'll trade you newscasts!

CATHY: Alright! Hang on to your hat! I had a meeting today with Johnny Nichols, the former Chamber of Commerce president, the one who first hired me.

MATT: Yeah! He's the guy who treated you to lunch quite regularly.

CATHY: Hey! Lunch is necessary for good health. *(Laughs)*

MATT: Did you have lunch today?

CATHY: Of course! You don't have a business meeting without lunch!

MATT: *(Resigned)* Of course not!. Business meeting?

CATHY: Yes! Johnny has been appointed a vice-president of the Star Bright Travel Division of Kal-Mart Enterprises, the big conglomerate.

MATT: Okay! I'm impressed. Yes! They'll soon own the world, maybe even half of China…

CATHY: Never mind! Now, when he heard I retired from the Chamber, he thought I should come aboard as regional director of his group travel division serving this whole part of the country. Think of it…a good salary, commission, expense account and traveling all over the world with groups of seniors living out their dreams or business executives at conventions.

MATT: Wait a minute! Wait a minute! I thought we retired.

CATHY: No! You retired! Remember? No more kids giving you the finger behind your back or making out in the back of the classroom during a biology lesson. If I heard that once, I heard it a thousand times…No more kids…

MATT: That's right! I was sick of it and glad to retire before they downsized the pension system…or I was ready for a sanitarium. What I want is a chance to relax, catch up on my reading, cultivate a hobby, maybe study music or just loaf as much as I want.

CATHY: Now, wait a minute! You're too young to retire that way. With my new job, we can do all kinds of things.

MATT: Look! I had 30 years on that treadmill and I'm too old to go traipsing around the world with a bunch of drunken conventioneers or souvenir-hunting seniors.

CATHY: Well, you may be too old, but I'm not! Me, I'm medium old and not too old to have fun and still get paid for it.

MATT: But, you'll never be home with a job like that.

CATHY: So, we'll make wherever we are our home!

MATT: But what about our kids and their kids... you know, our grandchildren?

CATHY: Now, listen mister! Our son Tim and his three kids are in Buenos Aires. Remember he's manager there for that big British bank.

MATT: I know, I know! His father-in-law is president of the bank that does business with the Argentinean orange growers...and with Tim's financial know-how, he's knocking the brains out of Florida's orange business.

CATHY: And we're paying two dollars a piece for oranges. You used to get a bushel for that money. So, anyway, Tim's doing alright for himself?

MATT: Hey! That's life nowadays. But there's Rory?

CATHY: Oh, yes! Our son who married a Spanish princess while he was touring Europe with that pro basketball team. What is she, the granddaughter to the third cousin of the second nephew of the late king? Am I right?

MATT: Hey! That's royalty enough for me!

CATHY: I'm impressed, your highness! Look, I'm proud of our kids, including Ned, the business manager for the pop singer, what's her name...Susan Sabrena. I wonder if they lip synch her television interviews. She's the toast of Japan and soon China. Another princess!

MATT: Look, he's making bundles of money and getting ready to set up a management firm for a bunch of tiny pop tarts and pretty boys who can't sing their way out of a paper bag. But they certainly sell one hell of a lot of CDs.

CATHY: Oh! I'm really proud of dear ol' Ned!

MATT: And you should be!!!

CATHY: But that's my point! The kids don't need us. They're happy in their own lives, their kids are well taken care of...what's to worry. Our lives are our own.

MATT: But you want to go all over the world! Humph! Now, I know where our kids' got their travel gene. Let them travel and send us e-mails or text messages or fancy Christmas presents. We have each other here at home, nice and quiet.

CATHY: But, I don't want nice and quiet! I want to do everything I dreamed of. Why should our kids have all the fun? Let's spend their inheritance. They're certainly aren't going to need what little we have.

MATT: But, the grandkids might!

CATHY: Oh, sure! Those kids probably have trust funds already. More power to them! Me, I want to enjoy life and what I can make of it. The world's mine to conquer. That's what Johnny said, and I agree!

MATT: Boy! Nichols sure sold you a bill of goods!

CATHY; And, what does that mean?

MATT: It means he's had his eye on you for years. Here's a chance to slip away with you on business trips and make up for lost opportunities in the past. Believe me, I know!

CATHY: Oh! You know! Why would Johnny want me? Listen, where he's at, he's tripping over all kinds of willing young women all the time! What chance would I have, even if I wanted it.

MATT: You never know until you come face-to-face with it.

CATHY: Oh! This is foolish and you know it. Look the new job is my news, and that's it! Now, what's yours!

MATT: Hardly as exciting as yours.

CATHY: Well, what is it?

MATT: Harry wants me to go to work for the school district.

CATHY: What do you mean, work for the school district? What happened to sitting and reading books, taking up a hobby?

MATT: The difference is that I'd work from home by computer as a grants writer for new programs at the school. The grants would include projects from kindergarten through high school. It's a great opportunity.

CATHY; But, what happened to sitting at home?

MATT: Hey! I can still stay at home, working from an office in our basement.

CATHY: But, what do you know about grant writing?

MATT: Look! I know the school system and there are courses at the university that I can take while I'm setting up shop. They'll pay me an advance against any grants I get. It's a win-win situation.

CATHY: But, you won't see the light of day for weeks at a time, working down in the basement.

MATT: Hey! We can still go to parties, the movies, dinner and some short trips. It'll be great!!

CATHY: Great? I've just got a job that can take us all over the world and you're willing to be happy with a dinner down the street or a movie a few miles from your basement.

MATT: Yes! I don't really want to do that much traveling. And, with the school district's offer, I can really do some good here right in town.

CATHY: Any other man in the world would jump at a chance to travel all over the world at virtually no cost with an exciting woman.

MATT: Exciting…?

CATHY: Me! Me! Stupid! Now, that's what I call a retirement plan.

MATT: Maybe it's a retirement plan for you or, for that matter, Johnny Nichols, but not for me.

CATHY: Now you're throwing Johnny Nichols in my face, just over some harmless lunches we had together when we both worked at the Chamber.

MATT: How do I know they were harmless?

CATHY: *(Angry)* You better know!

MATT: Alright, I was just jealous that's all. But, when you told me about getting this offer from Nichols, it just struck me wrong, especially at this time in our lives when we can be together more meaningfully.

CATHY: Meaningfully! With you holed up in the basement looking for money so those school kids can learn enough to work in future basements. That's meaningful?

MATT: That's ridiculous.

CATHY: You're damn right!

MATT: No, I didn't say the idea was ridiculous, only the way you describe it. Besides, I'd have to come upstairs for lunch and have it with you on the porch.

CATHY: Oh, now that's a pretty picture, me waiting for my big money man to come out of Fort Knox in the basement to sit with me for lunch that I would have to make. No way!!!

MATT: Didn't you always dream of being together when we retired.

CATHY: Yes, I did!

MATT: Well?

CATHY: I didn't mean in a basement. I saw us on a cruise ship, or in a five-star hotel or on sunny, sandy beaches.

MATT: That's not my idea of retirement, me running around in Hawaiian shirts and shorts.

CATHY: Listen! Don't knock the loud shirts and baggy shorts! They're the uniform of happiness.

MATT: Sure, the uniform for the bony knees brigade. No way!

CATHY: The kids would love it if we got to travel. Right now, their kids got more travel miles in a year than we got in our lifetime.

MATT: So they have to travel back to London and to Spain to see their relatives.

CATHY: And, they even do it alone. Why, Louisa will be going to prep school in England next year and Denise's son took golf lessons in South Carolina last summer. I tell you, I'm not about to let my grandkids rack up more travel miles than me. It was bad enough when our kids did it, but when their kids get more mileage points than we do, there's something wrong.

MATT: And, you think our kids and their kids would like to see us wandering around the world at our age.

CATHY: Of course they would. And, forget about age! It's just a number, not a guidepost!

MATT: That's easy for you to say.

CATHY: Well, it should be easy for you to say too.

MATT: Well, it's not!

CATHY: I have nothing else to say. I'm just not folding up because my birth certificate is brown around the edges.

MATT: Have you looked lately? It might be dust by now!

CATHY: *(Throws sofa pillow at him)* Now, you're skating on thin ice!

MATT: *(Moves towards upstage door)* Now, that could be a hobby! *(Starts down stairs)*

CATHY: *(Goes to door, and shouts after him)* That's right! Go down to your retirement dungeon!

(BLACKOUT)

Scene 1-2

(It is several days later. Cathy is on the phone with her friend Linda.)

CATHY: Yes, Linda! It's been three days now and Matt refuses to talk any more about my new job. He said I didn't even hint to him that I was thinking of working when he retired. No! You're right! He didn't tell me that he was thinking about being a consultant for the school district.

Yes, I called the kids to tell them about my new job. No! I didn't tell them that Matt didn't like the idea. They're really happy about my prospects and thought it would be wonderful for their old folks to traipse around the world.

Ned even suggested that his father become a roadie for one of his tiny tarts on a singing tour. Keeping her from getting busted for DWI. Wouldn't that be a blast! No! I can just see Matt at one of those concerts with 10,000 screaming teenagers. He'd find a bomb shelter to retire into!

Yes! He's serious about setting up an office in our basement to do grants writing for the school he couldn't wait to leave. Go figure!

Yeah! You better put that cruise on hold for the four of us, unless I can flood the basement. Now, I've got to drop it on him that I have to attend a travel seminar in Boston. I'll call you!

(Hangs up phone as Matt comes out of basement, wearing a carpenter's apron. He's obviously been working on his office)

MATT: Well, I added that paneling near the desk and put in a plug to bring in power for the computer, the printer and the copier.

CATHY: *(Sarcastically)* Well, you should be very proud of yourself. Maybe you can do a Mr. Fix-it television show right from your desk in between writing out grants.

MATT: Hey, maybe I could! Listen, it's comfortable and it's really going to work efficiently.

CATHY: I'm so happy for you.

MATT: Whom were you talking to?

CATHY: An almost client! Linda down the street! I told her about your retirement hobby.

MATT: Hey! It's not a hobby. It's a part-time job that gives me plenty of opportunity to do the things I always wanted to do..

CATHY: I know...reading, listening to music and gazing at the stars...

MATT: Don't be smart! It's the perfect set-up!

CATHY: If you were single!

MATT: What does that mean?

CATHY: Simple! Your plan doesn't include me.

MATT: Well, you plan doesn't include me.

CATHY: Well, it could. You could travel all over the world with me.

MATT: Wouldn't that be a little uncomfortable for our friend, Johnny Nichols.

CATHY: Not a bit, I'm sure that he'll have more than adequate companionship.

MATT: Wouldn't that make you jealous?

CATHY: You're crazy! Johnny and I work together. That's all! But, if you want it otherwise, maybe I can get a nip and tuck and give it a try!

MATT: I'm serious!

CATHY: So, am I!

MATT: Wait until the kids hear about this!

CATHY: Hey! Tim wants us to come down to Argentina. We'll never have to buy oranges again! And Rory'll try to work out a coronation we can attend. As for Ned, he even suggested you baby-sit some of those spaced-out teen singers he represents.

MATT: You mean, you've told them about our problem.

CATHY: No! I just told them about my new job and they thought it was wonderful for both of us.

MATT: You didn't tell them I didn't like it?

CATHY: No! You tell them yourself! I can hear them telling their kids about grandpa locking himself up in a basement. Maybe they can make it into a bedtime story about the old man in a dungeon planning to change the world, one schoolbook at a time.

MATT: Now, you're being ridiculous!

CATHY: I'm ridiculous! Hah! Our grandkids will have a field day with this situation. With their text messages, you'll be famous all over the world.

MATT: Yeah! And wait until they get a cell photo of grandma doing the hula in her Hawaiian grass skirt.

CATHY: Yeah! Maybe Ned can get me a job as the singing, swinging granny doing a pole-dancing hula.

MATT: *(Moves to basement door)* You're crazy!!!

CATHY: *(Looking down basement door)* I'm crazy! Look who's working in his own grants tomb.

(BLACKOUT)

Scene 1-3

(Several days later, Matt is on the phone in living room)

MATT: So, you think it's great for your mother to be flying and sailing all over the world. Ned, you've been with those so-called singers of yours too long. That's no retirement plan...selling trips, organizing them and then going with the groups to all sorts of places. Oh! You still think it's great for your mother to have such a wonderful job, do you? Well, for your information, she never consulted me or asked my opinion before she took the job.

Who offered her the job? That guy she used to work with, a Johnny Nichols. He's the guy. What? No, he's not your mother's lover!!! Watch your mouth! I admit I was jealous when she worked with him at the Chamber but I thought when she planned to retire from that job, there'd be no other contact. And, now this happens. What do you mean I can trust your mother? Well, I want to! But this all came so sudden.

Oh! You talked to Tim and Rory about it and they also think it's all right for your mother to go flying all over the world. Well, it's your fault, that's who!. She's jealous of all your traveling and living in other countries. No! I didn't say I actually blame you...but, she's still jealous of you kids and even, of your kids. Can you imagine? No, it's not funny! Boy, you're a big help. I thought you'd see my side of it. Now, don't get smart...the basement's fine.. What? Oh! I have no place to go but up! Ha! Ha! Real funny! Why did I think I'd get any sympathy from you! Okay! I know you think I'm the best father I the world. Thanks! What? Oh, I'm stodgy, am I?

Well, thanks a lot. Goodbye! *(Hangs up as Cathy enters front door with packages)* What's with the packages?

CATHY: It's some clothes I bought for the Boston seminar about next year's schedule of trips. It's a major conference. I needed something new to wear.

MATT: You've got a couple of closets of clothes upstairs. In fact, you even have part of my closet.

CATHY: Listen! Do you think I could go to this major meeting in an old outfit? Be real, will you!

MATT: You know, I thought you were kidding about going to Boston. I suppose what's his name is going!

CATHY: What's his name?

MATT: You know, that Johnny Nichols.

CATHY: Of course, he's going. He's a vice-president in the corporation, isn't he?

MATT: Oh! I forgot. Are you going to have your own room?

CATHY: Of course, I will. You don't think he'd give up his closet space, do you! Now, get off the Johnny Nichols bit. I told you, it's strictly business.

MATT: I wonder how many other retired wives are going to that meeting.

CATHY: Well, I know at least one retired husband who could go, if he weren't so stubborn! I've told you that you can go on trips with me.

MATT: Oh, good! I can take a tour around Boston while you're at meetings.

CATHY: Don't forget Fanuel Hall, it's very historic!

MATT: No thanks! I intend to be busy with my own business.

CATHY: That's right! I forgot! You need to be in your dungeon.

MATT: Well, at least I have my own phone number. I won't need to use the house phone for business.

CATHY: *(Mock seriousness)* Oh! Now we're having a trial telephonic separation?

MATT: Don't push! Don't push! *(Starts down basement)*

CATHY: Don't tempt me! don't tempt me! *(Makes motions that she's pushing him down stairs)*

(BLACKOUT)

Scene 1-4

(It's a week later. Cathy is on phone with Linda, a suitcase is sitting next to her)

CATHY: Oh! It was a wonderful trip! The other tour supervisors are a great bunch and full of ideas. We're selling a 10-day cruise from Miami into the Caribbean and then through the Panama Canal. It sounds great and it's a brand new ship that carries 3,000 passengers.

Yes! We have a great potential to sell plenty of cabins. I still wish I could convince Matt to go with me. It's a freebie and I think he'd love it.

No! I just got in as you were calling. I haven't seen Matt yet. I was hoping he'd pick me up at the airport after I called him from Boston to tell him what flight I was on.

No! Nothing's wrong, really! He's just miffed about my taking charge of my life and doing things I really wanted to do. He'll get over it and then things will be all right. It's happened over the years.

No! I'm not being complaisant about it. I love the guy and I know he loves me, so there's no problem there. It's just a matter of adjusting to our own ideas of retirement.

Let's get together for lunch later in the week. Good! 'Bye!

(Hangs up phone, goes to basement and calls downstairs)

Matt! I'm home. I thought you were going to pick me up at the airport. It cost me 30 dollars for a cab. Did you hear me?

MATT: *(From basement)* I'm sorry Cathy, I was on the phone all morning and I couldn't get away. I tried to phone you on your cell but I couldn't make the connection.

CATHY: Well, it's all right! I'm home now. Come on up. I have a present for you from Boston.

(She crosses to her suitcase, starts to take out package)

(Matt comes out of the basement)

MATT: *(Touch of sarcasm)* That was good of you to think of me while you were away.

CATHY: Now, don't start that. Didn't I call you every morning to say "good morning" and every night to say "good night."

MATT: Yes, you did!

CATHY: So, there! I was thinking about you while I was away.

MATT: You didn't call me at lunchtime.

CATHY:*(Sarcastically sympathetic)* I know, and I'm sorry! That was the time we were supposed to have lunch every day when you came up from the basement to eat what I had prepared you.

MATT: Don't be sarcastic!

CATHY: Who's sarcastic? Listen, I thought of you while I was away and wished you were there with me.

MATT: As it turned out, I was busy too! There's some action in the grants writing business, especially since I've gotten some help from the university.

CATHY; Oh! They did have a class after all!

MATT: No! But, they told me about someone who could help me while I'm learning the ropes.

CATHY: That's good! What's his name?

MATT: Maryanne!

CATHY: Maryanne?

MATT: Yes, she's a graduate student who's working on her doctorate.

CATHY: Graduate student? That makes her in her twenties then!

MATT: Yes, I'd say so!

CATHY: And, she's attractive too!

MATT: Yes, I'd say so!

CATHY: Well, then you have to spend some time at the university to work with her!

MATT: No! Not really!

CATHY: Not really!

MATT: No, I put another desk down in the basement!

(He exits down to basement as Cathy turns in shock)

(BLACKOUT)

Scene 1-5

(It is moments later and Cathy is on the phone with Linda)

CATHY: Yes, Linda! He just told me he has a young student working with him in the basement, a girl. Can you believe it? Did you know about that! Oh! You thought you saw a young blonde going into the basement door yesterday morning. You didn't see her leave, you say. Oh! You were out most of the afternoon until after dinner. Come to think of it, I didn't even ask if she's down there now. What do you mean, don't do anything hasty. Look, I'm not crazy but if I had a gun right now, I'd be taking aim. How could he hire a young blonde to work with him after all the junk he's been tossing at me for working with Johnny Nichols. Oh! You think that's why he's hired a young blonde. Well, we'll see about this! No! I won't do anything foolish. *(Afterthought)* Explain foolish! Never mind. I'll calm down first. Talk to you later. *(Hangs up phone, walks to basement door)*

(Sweetly) Matt, do you mind coming up stairs for a minute!

MATT: Just a minute, hon!

CATHY: *(Emphatic)* Make it now, hon!

(Matt appears at door)

MATT: Hey! I just remembered, you didn't give me the present you brought from Boston.

CATHY: Never mind! Let's first talk about the present you've given me.

MATT: What present?

CATHY: The blonde down in the basement.

MATT: Oh! Maryanne!

CATHY: Yes! Maryanne!

MATT: Yes! I'd like you to meet her. A really nice girl and smart too!

CATHY: Oh! I'll bet she is. Okay! Why don't you introduce me?

MATT: I can't now!

CATHY: Why not?

MATT: Because she just comes here in the morning. She has to teach classes at the university in the afternoon.

CATHY: Well, isn't that wonderful. *(Sarcastically)* Do you think she could stay for lunch some day?

MATT: *(Misses sarcasm)* Sure! That would be nice.

CATHY: Wouldn't it though! Maybe I could have Johnny Nichols over and we could have a foursome for lunch.

MATT: *(Picks up on sarcasm)* That would be nice too!

CATHY: What are you trying to do, having a blonde 20-year old come to the house while I'm out at work or maybe traveling for several days?

MATT: She's not 20!

CATHY: Oh, no!

MATT: No, she's 26!

CATHY: Oh, well that's different. Excuse me for being upset!

MATT: Why are you upset anyway?

CATHY: What will the neighbors think when they see a young woman come to the house every day.

MATT: It's only three mornings a week!

CATHY: Well, that sounds better...in a pig's eye!

MATT: Wait a minute! Are you accusing me of fooling around with that young girl.

CATHY: That young girl is a woman and from what Linda says, an attractive woman.

MATT: What's Linda got to say about this?

CATHY: Well, she's my friend and she saw your blonde coming into this house yesterday.

MATT: Oh! I didn't know Linda was a member of the Neighborhood Watch!

CATHY: Don't be smart. She didn't even want to tell me.

MATT: Cathy, there's nothing to tell.

CATHY: Then, why didn't you tell me when I phoned you this past week.

MATT: Maybe I thought you wouldn't understand and you'd be upset!

CATHY: Well, I guess you figured that right! Of course, I'd be upset and I'm upset now. What happened to your retirement plans....reading books, listening to music, sitting around relaxing.

MATT: I kind of see things differently now.

CATHY: Oh! I bet you do.

MATT: Now, listen here Cathy, if you're accusing me of fooling around with this young woman, you're howling up the wrong tree!

CATHY: My, you have a way with words! Listen! I'm not happy with this Maryanne of yours!

MATT: And, I guess I'm not happy about this Johnny of yours.

CATHY: Well, why don't we introduce them and maybe they'll run off together.

MATT: Cathy! Be serious! Anyway, I don't think she'd like him.

CATHY: Oh! You know her that well, do you?

MATT: Well, there are people you feel you know the moment you look into their eyes.

CATHY: Now, you're looking into her eyes?

MATT: Cathy, you know what I mean!

CATHY: I don't think I know anything you mean now! You should have stayed teaching and letting the kids give you the finger behind your back. Believe me, I know how they feel.

MATT: Now, be reasonable and don't get yourself all upset.

CATHY: Who's upset? I'm not upset! I'm just mad.

MATT: Look! I have to back down to the office. I'm expecting some phone calls. We'll talk later! *(Starts to basement door, opens it and then has afterthought)* By the way, what's the present?

CATHY: *(Reaches into suitcase and pulls out gift)* Here! An authentic replica of what they used to sign the Declaration of Independence. You know what you can do with it! *(Hands it to him as he ponders her suggestion while she storms out of the room)*

(BLACKOUT)

End of Act One

"Free at Last"
ACT TWO

Scene 2-1

(Matt is on phone with Harry)

MATT: I tell you Harry, it's been hell here this past week. Cathy is still upset. I introduced her to Maryanne Tuesday morning and there were icicles hanging off the drapes. No, there was no argument. Maryanne was very outgoing while Cathy was coolly cordial. Very coolly! I don't think Cathy quite understood Maryanne's enthusiasm and bubbling personality especially when she said that it was an honor working with me. "I'm sure I'll learn a lot from Matt!," she said. And, Cathy corrected her by saying "You mean Mr. Michaels!" "That's right, Mr. Michaels," Maryanne replied as if she were talking to a child. I could see the blood come up Cathy's cheeks and even to her scalp. I ended the conversation as quickly as I could and Maryanne went down to the office saying: "How wonderful it was to meet you Cathy!" and Cathy called after her: "Mrs. Michaels!"

I tell you Harry, it's been pretty tense around here all week. Cathy told me that from now on I have to go to the university to work with "what's her name" as she calls her. That takes away all the advantages of working in my own home.

No, I don't see Cathy's point! It's a perfectly innocent arrangement. But Cathy doesn't see it that way. What! What do you mean take the wind out of Cathy's sails! How! Go with her on the cruise? Are you kidding? Either she'll throw me overboard or I'll jump, one of the two. No way!

I know it's only 10 days but I'd be giving into her. I've got to be firm about this or the rest of my life will be hell on wheels. What? It's hell on wheels now?

But, how can I be cooperative now! The damage is done! You don't think so! You say, have one of my sons be the intermediary? But, which one? You think the one who works with the kid singers. He knows how to work with temperamental women. Do you think he'll do it? Maybe he could! What am I saying? I don't want to go cruising through the Panama Canal. Just this once, huh? I'll think about it!

Thanks for your understanding, Harry! You're a good friend...I hope!

(BLACKOUT)

Scene 2-2

(A day later. Cathy is on phone with Ned, her son)

CATHY: You say your father called you to intercede for him. Well, he can keep his old basement and his young assistant for all I care. What? He wants to go on the cruise with me now? You're kidding!!! What happened? Oh! He said he doesn't want to drive a wedge between us for the rest of our lives. Well, he seems to be getting smart. You say, his friend Harry suggested it to him. Well, there's a good friend even if I'd rather he didn't know all our business. You say, that's what friends are for!

But, Ned, I don't know if I want him to go on the cruise now. He's taken a lot of the fun out of it. Oh! You think I could make him like the trip if I forgive and forget...and what? Oh! I shouldn't pay too much attention to Johnny Nichols.

Is he still harping on that? Look, it's a business arrangement, that's all. Oh! You'd understand if it was more than that! Ned, you've been hanging around with those kinky kids too long! I'm not interested in any other man. But, I am interested in having an exciting time for the rest of my life and I just wish your father would want to share that with me. I'll even promise to visit him in his basement once in a while. In fact in a wild moment we could use his desk to make... never mind, you're too young!

Alright! I'll ask him one more time and not continue our previous arguments. I promise. Thanks for your help, Ned. Give my regards to the baby broads!

(Hangs up phone. Thinks a moment...then goes to basement door and calls to Matt)

CATHY: *(Sincere)* Matt! Would you come up here for a minute?

MATT: *(From basement)* You want me to come up?

CATHY: *(Trying to contain herself, sweetly)* Yes, Matt! I'd like to talk to you.

MATT: *(From basement)* Okay, Cathy, if you really want to talk to me.

CATHY: *(Controlling herself)* YES! I really want to talk with you... NOW!

MATT: *(Enters from basement door)* My, Cathy, you're looking lovely today.

CATHY: Oh! Today I look lovely? *(Catches her sarcasm, changes tone quickly)* Thank you Matt!

MATT: You're welcome. You do look lovely!

CATHY: Thank you again!

MATT: What did you want?

CATHY: Your son, the one with the stable of swinging singers, called me.

MATT: Oh, you mean Ned?

CATHY: Yes, Ned!

MATT: How's he doing?

CATHY: You must know! He said you called him yesterday.

MATT: Oh, yeah! That's right, I did!

CATHY: And he said that you had second thoughts about going on the cruise with me.

MATT: Well, I thought maybe if you REALLY wanted me to go with you, I could get away from the office for a couple of weeks.

CATHY: OH! You think you could bear to leave the basement and the blonde.

MATT: Now, Cathy! Let's not bring Maryanne into this situation again, please!

CATHY: You're right! Let's be civilized!

MATT: Thank you! Let's do!

CATHY: *(Politely)* Well, Matt, would you like to go with me on the cruise through the Panama Canal next week?

MATT: I think I'd be delighted.

CATHY: You THINK you'd be delighted.

MATT: I KNOW I'll be delighted!

CATHY: Alright, Matt! I'll make arrangements for your tickets for the trip and I'll get an upscale cabin for the two of us.

MATT: That would be nice. What should I pack?

CATHY: Make sure you have your summer tux and some comfortable clothes to stroll around the deck in the sunshine.

MATT: A summer tux?

CATHY: You need one for the Captain's dinner.

MATT: We're going to have dinner with the captain of the ship?

CATHY: Of course, on the second night at sea, the captain welcomes everybody on board.

MATT: I thought you said that this ship holds 3,000 passengers?

CATHY: It does!

MATT: That's a lot of handshaking!

CATHY: Well, I suppose we won't see the captain for the following two days...he'll have his hand soaking in ice.

MATT: Well, it's his hand!

CATHY: So, it's settled, then?

MATT: Aye, aye captain!

CATHY: Don't get smart!

MATT: Okay! I'll be good. Oh! By the way, I can take my laptop with me so I can keep current with my work. Maryanne suggested it!

CATHY: She knew you were going on this trip before I actually did?

MATT: No, not really! I just asked her if it was possible to keep in touch with her if I was traveling. I didn't mention any cruise or anything like that.

CATHY: And, she said it was possible.

MATT: Yes! And, she said the cell phone might be a way also.

CATHY: And, you're going to do some work while on board.

MATT: Well, that'll sort of be the best of all worlds...keeping up with my work while enjoying going on a cruise with you.

CATHY: You got it all figured out, haven't you?

MATT: Isn't it a good plan?

CATHY: *(Relents)* I suppose so!

MATT: Good! I'll pack tonight and get my tux pressed tomorrow. *(Turns to the basement door)*

CATHY: Where are you going now?

MATT: Back downstairs to catch up on my work. *(Goes downstairs)*

CATHY: *(Calls down to him)* Just promise me that on the cruise you won't set up a desk in the engine room.

BLACK OUT

Scene 2-3

(Shortly after previous scene, Cathy is on phone with Linda)

CATHY: That's right, Linda! Matt is going with me on the cruise and he seems to want to make an attempt to have fun. Yes! I'm really happy he's coming along and I hope that I can make it fun for him. And, maybe both of us can forget Maryanne and Johnny long enough to be ourselves. Who knows, maybe the Caribbean moonlight will awaken our mutual romantic interest in each other. Of course, I'm interested in him that way. I'm not that old, you know. Besides, I bought a strapless dress that may well knock his eyes out. Who? Why Matt of course. What would I have worn if Matt hadn't come on the cruise? A shawl!

Will Matt be up to it? My! You have a way with words. Wish me luck! I'll call you when I get back!

Now, I have to buy him a box of salt water Viagra! *(Hangs up)*

BLACKOUT

Scene 2-4

(Eleven days later)

(Matt's at the basement desk on phone with Harry. He's wearing a bathrobe and pajamas and looks disheveled.)

MATT: ...and then, I ate my first piece of solid food. That's right, I was sick for five days, that's deathly sick. For the rest of it I was only normally sick.

There were about 300 of us who got sick. No! Cathy didn't get sick, except of me being sick. They served some kind of South American dish that I tried. When about five people at the next table fell off their chairs from that food, they stopped serving it. Of course, I had finished my meal. Cathy had an English cut of prime rib and wound up healthy as a horse, or at least a Shetland pony.....

(LIGHTS /DIM ON BASEMENT PHONE)

(LIGHTS /COME UP ON LIVING ROOM PHONE)

CATHY: Yes! Sick as a dog for almost the whole trip. It was the Captain's Dinner...or what's became known as the Captain's Mess. They held it on the second night as we were approaching the Caribbean end of the Panama Canal. Matt staggered to bed and didn't get up again until we had returned from the Pacific side of the canal five days later. Then, he was just seasick!

What! No, we never got a chance to test the salt water Viagra....

(LIGHTS /REVERSE BETWEEN LIVING ROOM AND BASEMENT)

MATT: No! I don't know what they put in the DeBoef del Cocao. I think it was filet of Chilean mountain goat. I don't know except I don't think it'll be on any future menus unless they equip the ship with a bigger sick bay. Out of almost 3,000 passengers, I was among 300 people who got sick. What? No! I never did see Panama! I couldn't raise me head off the pillow during the whole passage in the Canal. No! No! They didn't offer to fly us home. That's all I would have needed....

(LIGHTS /REVERSE)

CATHY: I don't think I'll ever get him on an airplane again. Did I tell you they lost his luggage when we flew to Miami before the cruise. Yes! I tell you! They lost his luggage! I've never seen a grown man cry before. I had to drag him on board the ship. The airline gave him $300 to buy some clothes on shipboard. All he got for that was jeans, two Hawaiian shirts and a pair of loafers. The cruise line gave him a complimentary tuxedo rental on board for the Captain's Dinner. Can you guess the rest? Yes! He threw up all over it....

(LIGHTS /SWITCH)

MATT: I was a mess, a sick mess. They took me to the ship's infirmary and that was worse. Have you ever been with dozens of sick people, all suffering the same thing as you, gagging and retching. They got us back to our rooms once they calmed the upset stomachs and cleaned us up. Cathy slept on the cabin's sofa for the rest of the trip.....

(LIGHTS /SWITCH)

CATHY: I tried to sleep with him to comfort him but he didn't trust his stomach and said he didn't want to be remembered in his obituary that he threw up all over his wife in bed just before he died. "If the retching didn't kill me, you would!," he told me. He barely took notice that I was wearing a seductive and flimsy negligee. It was especially seductive, he said, when I was standing between him and the moonlight from the window but the only thing that came up was…his dinner.

(LIGHTS /SWITCH)

MATT: Yes! I felt 20 years older the way I looked and the way I felt. On the last day as we were approaching Miami, I did try walking on the deck with Cathy. But you had to know! This trip was star-crossed. The tail end of a hurricane caught up with us and we rocked-and-rolled our way into port. Fortunately, I hadn't eaten much and didn't have much to lose this time.

I was never so glad to see anything as when I saw the Miami skyline, stormy as it was…

(LIGHTS /SWITCH)

CATHY: I had to help him down the gangplank, even as he attempted to be the strong returned seafarer returning to port....you know the 19th century New England whaling man! When we got to the airport, they told us that they had found Matt's luggage and they would put it on our plane going back home. I think that's the only thing that got him to take the plane. He was all for taking a train back....

(LIGHTS /SWITCH)

MATT: Yes, I'm feeling a little better but I'm going to take it easy for another week or so in a place that's not rocking or taking off. No! I've asked Maryanne to send her stuff by e-mail and I'll do the same. She's too young to see a man looking like I do...Yes! That's true also, I don't want her to see me look this way....

(LIGHTS /SWITCH)

CATHY: What's next! Well, the Kal-Mar people thanked me for helping make their sick people comfortable and taking care of their needs while they were on board. They think I saved the big convention on board for next year by my attending to their employees, particularly four of their vice-presidents who got sick.

Johnny Nichols? Oh! He was fired! Yes, fired! They found out he was entertaining one of the vice-presidents' wives in his stateroom for several nights on board while her husband was sick. That's right, he was fired on the spot! At least they didn't make him walk the plank. ....

(LIGHTS /SWITCH)

MATT: Yes! There was one good thing that came out of the trip. Yes, one! The company fired this Johnny Nichols! Yeah! He was bedding one of the Kal-Mar vice-president's wives while the guy was in sick bay. She certainly was no Florence Nightingale, more like a camp follower. Anyway, I was pleased to know that he wasn't trying to make Cathy his night nurse. No! He didn't get sick. The guy drank too much liquor for any self-respecting germ to get to him. At least Cathy won't have to report to him anymore. I know! I know! I shouldn't have believed Cathy would have anything to do with Nichols…as a cabin companion. I was just jealous, that's all. Thanks for listening to my tale of woe. You're right! The trip cleared up my jealousy …and I what? Oh! Yes! The trip proved that I could work with Maryanne at a distance. E-mail is a wonderful salve for a jealous heart. No! I haven't told Cathy yet that Maryanne has to spend more time on campus with some extra teaching but can work with me by e-mail and fax. I'll see you! *(Hangs up, exits as if going upstairs)*

(LIGHTS /SWITCH)

CATHY: Well, at least Matt knows that Johnny Nichols didn't have me on his radar. Would you believe the woman he seduced was his immediate supervisor's wife. Talk about doing a high wire act without a net. Hey! Thanks for listening. Talk to you soon. *(Hangs up as Matt enters room from basement)* Are you feeling better?

MATT: I'm coming around. A few more days and I'll be my old relaxed self.

CATHY: Oh! Back to reading and relaxing!

MATT: No! I'm going to continue with the part time work as a grants writer.

CATHY: When does your blonde helper start back in the basement?

MATT: I'm assuming you mean Maryanne?

CATHY: Yes! I mean Mary whosis!

MATT: Well, while we were away, the university people asked her to take over some more classes. So, she'll only be able to work with me by phone, fax or e-mail!

CATHY: *(Mock sadness)* Ohhhhh!

MATT: That makes you sad, doesn't it?

CATHY: Not as long as it doesn't make you sad.

MATT: No! I really didn't work that long to get to know her well but, I'll admit, it was nice to have another woman think I was still capable of making some contribution to the community.

CATHY: Oh! And who's the other woman?

MATT: I was hoping that it was you!

CATHY: You did, huh? Well, I'll admit I was disappointed to hear that you had planned to just sit and vegetate for the rest of your life.

MATT: I know! But, when you told me what you wanted to do, it blew me away.

CATHY: I guess maybe I came on too strong! But, I do like the travel business.

MATT: Well, I suppose in moderation, it might work.

CATHY: And, in moderation, maybe you can work.

MATT: And, in between, we can do things together...in moderation!

CATHY: Like travel?

MATT: Not on airlines that lose luggage! Or ships that make food testers out of you!

CATHY: That could be arranged. What would you really like to do on a vacation...and don't tell me you want to just go sit somewhere!

MATT: You know, something I've always thought fascinating is that rail trip across Canada from Montreal to Vancouver.

CATHY: Yes! They say that's a great trip!!! Maybe not for groups but for two people, it could work! *(She takes step towards him)*

MATT: Maybe we could think about something like that. *(He moves to her)*

CATHY: It's a plan. And, then we can fly home from Vancouver! *(Takes his hands in hers)*

MATT: Well, I've always wanted to see Seattle! We could take a train to there from Vancouver! *(Starts to embrace her)*

CATHY: Yes, we could, if you'd like that, I think I could like it. *(Responds to his embrace)*

MATT: Then, we might take the train right down the California West Coast. *(Holds her closer)*

CATHY: Yes! *(Starts breathing heavily)* They do have trains that can do that! If you really want to! Do you?

MATT:*(Breathlessly)* As you said. It's a plan

CATHY: Well, how will we work if we travel? *(Breathing heavily)*

MATT: *(Kisses her neck)* There's laptops..and cell phones … and faxes! Home away from home!

CATHY: Oh! Sweetheart, I feel *(Nuzzles his ear)*..I've created a monster.

MATT: *(Kisses her neck)* It can be a retirement *(Catches his breath)* where we can practice…*(Breathless)* give and take.

CATHY: *(Really breathless)* Oh! Yes! Give and take! *(Kisses his neck)* As long as we both practice it equally.

M ATT: Yes, yes! Fifty-fifty! *(Kisses her cheek)*

CATHY: *(She kisses his cheek)* Ohhh! Right now, I'd take sixty-forty!

MATT: *(Kisses her forehead and then breathlessly)* How big.. how big are the bedrooms on trains!

CATHY: *(Breathy)* Big enough to have showers after…

MATT: *(Catching his breath)* And a picture window!

CATHY: I think so, why?

MATT: *(Now trying to catch his breath)* I'd like to see you at the window…gazing at the moon …. wearing your new negligee.

CATHY: *(Kittenish, purring)* You would?

MATT: *(Difficult breathing)* Yes, I would!!

CATHY: *(Puts her lips near his)* Then, I'll buy an extra one in case the trip gets really, really long. *(They kiss passionately to moderate dim out)*

END OF PLAY

"Double Trouble"

A New Play

By Martin P. Kelly

Note from the Author

One summer noontime between rehearsals at the Bridge Theater in Whitehall for one of our history plays, I was having lunch with a member of the board and, for whatever reason, he began telling me about his two younger brothers who were identical twins. When they were college students, my colleague said, one of them became friends with a college girl and was dating her during the summer on the Cape.

So, what was the story? Well, when the dating twin was busy, he urged his brother to take his place and he did. So, close were the twins' personalities and physical appearances that the young lady never knew the difference.

Later, that night I thought about the story and jotted down a brief outline on a scrap of paper..

Within the next two weeks, I had sketched out and then completed the following play.

It amused me to write it and hope that it amuses you in reading it and/or performing it.

As you may notice, only two actual actors are used in the play, even though there are four characters. This hopefully makes the play a challenge for the actors as well as the director. It can also provide a need for athletic dressers in the quick changes required while also offering producers a small cast to recruit. Enough said!

MPK

"Double Trouble"
ACT ONE

Time: The present

Location: A large city

Setting: The stage consists of two living rooms with a shared center that contains a sofa and a coffee table that represent those items in each of the two distinct apartments. There are doors at stage right and stage left that lead into a bedroom in each apartment. Doors up right center and left center are entrances to the apartments. The apartments are actually in different parts of the city.

The apartment on stage right belongs to Holly Lawrence while the apartment on stage left belongs to Jack Kingsworth. Both characters are in their early thirties, both are attractive people with active careers. Holly's a dress designer and Jack's an architect. They know each other and date occasionally. Both are open to romance but are cautious about committing.

HOLLY: *(Enters up right door as phone is ringing, she drops upscale shopping bag and rushes to phone)*

Hello! Oh! It's you, Ruthie! Where are you? In town! Really! That's great, we'll get together. How long are you going to be here? A week! You're staying at the Marriott! Wonderful! How are things in Chicago? That bad! I'm kidding. Any romance going on for you! Not enough time!

Me? Well, there's an architect I see for dinner once in a while. He works downtown in the building next to mine. Yes, about my age! A romance? Well, he doesn't seem ready to commit and I'm not sure I am. After all, I'm in and out of town as much as he is. Several manufacturers have bought my dress designs so I have to attend the shows and deal with buyers as part of my royalty arrangement. Keeps me hopping!

And Jack's work…Yes, that's his name..Jack! Hey! It's easy to remember!

Anyway, his work takes him out of town a lot, especially at present with his firm's contract for a major office building in Boston.

Listen, I have to attend a dinner meeting tonight but I want to see you afterwards. I'll leave the key under the doormat, scotch taped to the bottom. Tricky, huh? Great! I'll see you later.

(Hangs up, exits into bedroom at right)

JACK: *(Enters stage left upstage door, flicks lights on and drops brief case on table, goes to cabinet down left and pours himself a drink. Then, picks up phone and dials. Phone rings in the stage right apartment. Holly enters wearing robe, she picks up phone and says "Hello!".)*

Holly! It's Jack! Yes! I just got in but have to rush right out for drinks with a couple of clients in from Boston. It shouldn't be too long. I'd like to drop in tonight if you're not too tired. I have something very important to tell you

HOLLY: *(Somewhat hesitant)* Well, I'm on my way out in a few minutes to go to dinner. A couple of manufacturers' reps!

JACK: *(Emphatic)* I'd really like to see you!

HOLLY: Is it really that important?

JACK: It really is important!

HOLLY: Can't it wait until tomorrow night?

JACK: It could! But, I'd rather talk about it with you tonight!

HOLLY: *(Relents)* Well, I guess it's alright. I shouldn't be too late.

JACK: That's great. See you later. *(Hangs up, exits into bedroom stage left)*

HOLLY: *(Hangs up phone, talks to herself)* If truth be told, I'd like to see him too! But, this is a surprise! What can be so important? Well, I'll soon find out later! *(Starts into bedroom, then turns.)* Oh, sh...! Ruthie will be here sometime tonight. I better call Jack back *(starts to phone, stops)* No! He might as well meet her. She won't be here until I get home. *(Enters bedroom, taking off robe as lights go down on stage right)*

JACK: *(Enters from left bedroom with different jacket over his arm. He checks his French cuffs and then puts on the jacket, picks up phone, dials)*

Phillip! This is Jack Kingsworth. I'm meeting some clients at your lounge in a few minutes. Give me an hour with them and then call me on my cell phone so I can make an excuse to get away. I have an important date tonight that could mean a lot to me. *(Smiles)* No! It's nothing like that! That's right! Serious! Thanks.

(Hangs up phone, checks mirror and exits out stage left door as lights go down, leaving full stage in dim light.)

(An hour passes.)

(Soon we hear a rustling outside Holly's door, then a key in the lock and as the door opens, the woman turns on the light. It is Holly...no...it's Ruth, Holly's twin sister, a dead on image of Holly, who takes scotch tape off the key and puts the key on the table. She takes off her coat, checks the bedroom, moves to sofa and then remembers and goes to the phone, and dials.)

RUTHIE: Hello! Mom! It's Ruthie! I'm in town. Yes, it was a rough flight from Chicago. We had head winds all the way. Like I told you, I'll be here for a week. I'm staying at the Marriott. I left you the number. Stay with Holly? No, her apartment's too small for me to stay here with both of us trying to get to work. Besides, I have an expense account! Speak to her? Well, she's out to a dinner but she left me a key to let myself in.

Yes, it's a nice place. I know she's never invited you but she will. As I said it's small. She's a very busy woman, like the rest of us. Settle down? Me? Mom, how can I settle down when I'm on the road all the time? Get off the road, you say, stay put, find a man, have a family. I know, Mom! My clock's ticking. No! I'm not meeting a man during the week. The trip's all business.

Mom, I have to freshen up before Holly gets here. I'll call you tomorrow morning. Yes, I'll have Holly call you too!

(Hangs up phone, looks at it) Mom, don't ever change! I wouldn't know what to do if you didn't goad me into greatness! *(Slight laugh)* Get off the road, have a family...in time, in time... *(She exits into stage right bedroom as lights dim. A half hour passes)*

(Ruthie's doorbell rings. Ruthie enters room and looks at door as doorbell rings again. She goes to door and opens it. Jack's standing there.)

JACK: Oh! Holly! I'm glad you're here. You finished dinner in good time. That's good!

(He enters)

RUTH: Dinner? Wha..?

JACK: Your manufacturing reps! Did you use the cell phone bit to get away. That's what I did with my clients. I got the contract and escaped the small talk. So, here I am. *(Makes move towards "Holly")*

RUTH: *(Backs away, puzzled)* Yes! Cells phones are a wonder!

JACK: Were you wondering why I wanted to talk to talk to you tonight?

RUTH: Tonight!!!

JACK: Yes! I phoned you a couple of hours ago to see if I could come over tonight....Remember?

RUTH: *(Confused but decides to play along)* Oh, yes! Of course! I guess my mind's still with my clients.

JACK: Well, let's forget clients! *(takes her hand and leads her to the sofa)* Here, sit down! *(She does tentatively)*

RUTH: But, there's something I better tell you...

JACK: *(Emphatically)* Me first!

RUTH: But, I really…*(Jack raises his hand to stop her talking, she agrees tentatively)* You first!

JACK: You know we've been going out for about a year now to dinner and an occasional show.

RUTH: *(Playing along as in a game)* Has it been a year already?

JACK: *(Laughs)* Of course, I checked my calendar.

RUTH: *(Parries)* It seems only like minutes ago!

JACK: Well, no matter! *(Eases towards her on the sofa as she backs away)* Here's the news! I've been offered a great job with the company at its Chicago office…

RUTH: Chicago?

JACK: Yes, can you imagine! Me, Jack Kingsworth, working with the top brass!

RUTH: *(Points at him)* Oh! *(now it all comes together)*…Jack!

JACK: Yes, me Jack! You know I've had to report there occasionally. Well, they've been impressed with what I've done in the last several years, especially on their Boston building.

RUTH: *(Politely)* That's wonderful…Jack!

JACK: I have to move to Chicago within a month!

RUTH: *(Acts surprised)* A month you say!

JACK: I know that this is short notice but I've found myself wondering all day how I would feel working in Chicago.

RUTH:*(Reassuring)* Oh! You'll like Chicago!

JACK: But, you'd still be here! I'm not sure I can go without you!

RUTH: *(Anxious)* You what? Go without me?

JACK: Holly! I hoped you'd feel the same as I do. You must know that I've felt close to you and fond of you..

RUTH: You do?

JACK: *(With emphasis)* Yes! And even in love with you.

RUTH: *(Really surprised)* In love!

JACK: Yes! Didn't you have any idea?

RUTH: I don't know what to say!

JACK: Holly tell me that you feel the same way.

RUTH: *(Trying to work her way out of the moment)* I r-e-a-l-l-y don't know what to say.

JACK: I know that it's a lot of news in so short a time.

RUTH: I'll say. *(Makes up her mind)* Look, I've got to tell you something....

JACK: Just tell me that you love me and you'll go with me...

RUTH: Go with you..?

JACK: Yes! *(takes her into his arms and kisses her)*

RUTH: *(Rises flustered, crosses to right)* Whew! Now, I'm telling you, I need to tell you something.

JACK: *(Rises, crosses to her)* Just tell me you love me and will go with me.

RUTH: But, I really have to...

JACK: I know, your dress design business. But you can do that anywhere, here, Chicago, Boston, anywhere!

RUTH: *(Getting more flustered)* Oh, yes! My dress design business.

JACK: I won't be taking you away from anything! You can still keep your clients and business associates while we have each other.

RUTH: *(Now curious, decides to string out the moment)* But, Chicago!

JACK: Didn't you tell me once that you lived in Chicago.

RUTH: I do! I mean, I did!

JACK: Then, it's a win-win situation. We'll have each other, we'll both have our work in Chicago where I'm sure you have friends or brothers or sisters.

RUTH: *(Now caught up in a whirlwind)* Yes… sister!

JACK: What could be better?

RUTH: Jack! *(surprised at saying his name)* Jack! This has come at me so fast, that I don't what or how to say it.

JACK: Look! I know that this is a surprise to you…

RUTH: Yes, it's a surprise alright!

JACK: *(Being reasonable)* Look! I'll leave now and call you later after you've got a chance to think it over. All right!

RUTH: *(Sees escape from situation)* Yes, yes! I can think it over.

JACK: *(Embraces her again, kisses her, and goes to door)* I know we can be happy….I'll call later. *(Exits, blowing her a kiss)*

RUTH: Oh, my God! What the hell just happened here? Holly never told me this guy was serious! I wonder if she had any idea. Why didn't I tell him I'm not Holly. How could he not know? *(She looks in mirror and holds up a picture of Holly)* Damn, I can't even tell the difference. Oh! I've got to call Holly and tell her. *(Starts for phone)* Wait a minute! What am I going to tell her? That I've been making out with her boyfriend! *(Makes decision, picks up phone, dials)* Oh! Holly, I hope the cell phone didn't disturb your dinner. You were just breaking up anyway! Good! Oh, I called to tell you that…What? Oh, yes! I'm at your apartment but *(thinks a moment)* I…I…I've been called back to a meeting with another set of manufacturers' reps. I'm sorry. I'll replace the key under the mat! We'll have lunch tomorrow! I'll call! Thanks! *(Hangs up phone, takes deep breath, goes to the mirror, checks her hair and lipstick and then picks up the key, rewraps it in scotch tape, heads for the door, looks back at the sofa, shakes her head and then exits after she flips off the lights)*

(About a half hour later)

(Holly enters, flips on lights and puts key on the table)

HOLLY: *(Goes to phone, dials)* Hello Mom! Yes, I've heard from Ruthie! Oh, she called...from my apartment. That's right! How does she look to me? I don't know. I didn't see her! Yes, we were supposed to meet here! No, we didn't have an argument. Mom, she phoned me at the restaurant where I was having dinner and told me she was called back to a meeting. We'll meet for lunch tomorrow. *(Repeating mother's words)* Oh, it's too bad we're too busy to visit with each other....and their mother! That's not it, Mom! We're in demanding professions. Too demanding, you say! Well, it's all your fault and Dad's. After all, you put us through college and encouraged us to make our way in the world. No, Mom, don't cry. I didn't mean to sound ...mean! Honest, Ruthie and I will do better. After all, she does live in Chicago near you and Dad. *(Again repeating mother)* She should be home with her parents. Mom, she's thirty-two years old and so am I, if you remember! *(Repeats mother)* We arrived in this world together. Oh! I was first...by two minutes. That makes Ruthie my younger sister. No, Mom, I'm not being a smartass! Look, Mom, I've got to get to bed...I have a full day of work tomorrow. Yes, I'll make time to have lunch with Ruthie. Goodnight, Mom, I love you! And you love me. That's good. Thanks, Mom! *(Hangs up, shaking her head, exits into bedroom)*

(Phone rings, Holly comes out of bedroom) Hello! Yo just got to the restaurant. I thought we were going to meet tomorrow morning! You need to see me tonight! Alright! *(Hangs up phone)* Dress manufacturers!!! They really call the shots! *(Checks her hair, grabs coat and keys and exits door)*

(A few minutes later, Jack enters his apartment stage left, still on a high. Takes off his jacket, answers the ringing phone)

JACK: Pete! What a surprise. You're coming back to New York from London! That's great. I've been jealous. Two months in London on an expense account, wining and dining clients, and I expect, dating some willing young women interested in an American bank executive. Listen, let me tell you the news! Tonight, I kind of proposed to Holly. Holly? Oh, she's the girl I've been going out with...Yes, I kind of proposed! I told her about my promotion. Yes! Yes! I've been named assistant vice-president for client relations and have to move to Chicago. Thanks! The promotion was a surprise for me too but I have to move there in a month. That's right! It's a quick move so that's why I went over to Holly's apartment tonight to tell her. Then I suggested that she go with me to Chicago. No, it wasn't a marriage proposal exactly but it's implied. What? A marriage proposal is never implied to a woman! Well, I'm building up to it. Pete, you'll have to meet her. After all, you're my brother! You have vacation time! That's great. Why don't you fly here and meet Holly. You'll see why I'm so excited. Wonderful! Call me and let me know when you can come up here. Good night..or good morning, whatever time it is over there! *(Hangs up phone)* Now, he knows so there's no turning back or he'll never let me hear the end of it for the rest of my life.

(Turns off light and goes into bedroom)

(Stage lights dim to denote an hour passing)

(Lights come up on Holly's apartment shortly)

HOLLY: *(Sings to herself as she takes off jacket and begins getting ready to take a shower)* I didn't plan on that other rep arriving tonight. I'm glad now that Ruthie had to go back to a meeting. I'm not up to having her meet Jack tonight. Oh! I forgot! Jack's coming over in a little while. Damn! I better call him and ask him to postpone coming over tonight. It's 8:30 already and I'm really tired. He certainly sounded enthusiastic about telling me something. But, it'll have to wait. *(Goes to phone and dials)*

(Phone rings in Jack's apartment and after a few moments, he comes out of bedroom, flicks on lights and picks up phone. He's wearing a robe.)

JACK: Hello!

HOLLY: Jack, I just wanted to tell you…

JACK: Oh, Holly..I'm thrilled you called me so fast!

HOLLY: What!!!

JACK: I didn't dare hope that you'd make up your mind this quickly. Oh! I hope you've called to say "yes!"

HOLLY: Say "yes"? I called to say that I'm really too tired to talk to you tonight.

JACK: Well, I said that I'd expect you'd need time to think over my proposition.

HOLLY: Proposition? Jack, what are you talking about?

JACK: Holly! The one I told you about a couple of hours ago at your apartment.

HOLLY: A couple of when at my what!!!!

JACK: Don't you remember! Oh, Holly! Don't tell me that I confused you with my enthusiasm.

HOLLY: "Confused" is a word for this conversation.

JACK: Why, I told you about my new job offer in Chicago!

HOLLY: You did?

JACK: And, I asked you to come with me to Chicago. You don't remember?

HOLLY: *(Now thoroughly confused)* I'm sorry, my meetings were involved and maybe my mind has gone blank.

JACK: You don't remember me kissing you…!

HOLLY: Kissing me????

JACK: Yes! I couldn't help myself. It was a magic moment for me!

HOLLY: Magic!!!

JACK: I was amazed that I had the nerve to ask you to come with me to Chicago.

HOLLY: To Chicago?

JACK: Where my new job will be!

HOLLY: I'm sorry! This is all too confusing for me. You say you came over to my apartment and, in a word, proposed that I come to Chicago with you.

JACK: Yes! Tell me you remember! Oh, I know that what I said and did might have been confusing to you. In fact, I have to admit that you did seem confused and that's why I wanted you to think about it. I didn't expect that you'd get back to me so soon. I couldn't be happier.

HOLLY: I'm happy you're happy but I need some time to consider our current conversation. Let me call you tomorrow. I must be too sleepy to digest this conversation.

JACK: Sure, Holly! Like I told you earlier, I love you...

HOLLY: Love me?

JACK: Yes, love you! Maybe I was too enthusiastic and left you confused. Please do as I suggested earlier...think it over tonight and let's talk tomorrow.

HOLLY: Yes, yes! Let's talk tomorrow! Call me! *(Hangs up, shaking her head, thoroughly confused)* What in the world is he talking about? He told me that he loved me...he kissed me....he wants me to go to Chicago with him..he...I don't know what to think!*(Thinks a minute, then appears shocked)* It couldn't be...no, that wouldn't happen. *(Picks up phone and dials)* Are you still at your meeting. Oh! You're in your hotel room. Good! Now, listen. I just had a very confusing conversation with Jack..yes, Jack, remember the guy I go out with. He said that he met me at my apartment a few hours ago and that he sort of proposed to me and wanted me to go to Chicago with him because he got a new job. That's right! How could he have done that. I wasn't at my apartment a few hours ago. *(Now, it really dawns on her)* Wait a minute! Ruthie! Did he come here while you were here? Tell me, did he come over and mistake you for me? He did! And, why didn't you tell him you're my sister..twin sister? Oh! he wouldn't let you get a word in edgeways! But, you had time to kiss him. Don't deny it. He told me he kissed me but I wasn't here, you were! So, is he a good kisser? Oh!, you didn't kiss him, he kissed you! *(Sarcastically)*

Well, that's different. Like hell it is! . Oh! Nothing else happened. You didn't encourage him to kiss you. How about the proposal to go to Chicago? Oh, it surprised you. Tell me, you didn't accept on my behalf. That's good. I won't have to pack right away. Listen, Ruthie, I know people have been confused all our lives about our resemblance to each other and I know we've done things to confuse the boys in high school. But, Ruthie, this is real life. *(Listens)* And, just how are you going to explain it to him? Look, I'm not going to have Jack thinking that I'm considering going to Chicago with him. I like the guy but I'm not sure… Never mind that he seems to be a nice guy. That's for me to decide. Oh, I'm lucky to have a man like Jack in love with me, am I? Maybe so, but I would have liked to have heard it first hand! *(Listens)* Oh, Ruthie! I got to believe you wouldn't do anything to hurt me deliberately. But, I've got to straighten this thing out. Right! But how can I straighten it out without having to give him an answer about Chicago? Oh, I've got to think this out clearly. I've got to sleep on it. *(Listens)* Yes, we'll both sleep on it. No, Ruthie, I don't hate you. After all you're my younger sister. Never mind, just ask Mom. Goodnight Ruthie! Yes, I love you. And you do too. Thanks, goodnight!

(Hangs up)

(Lights dim. They come up in Holly's apartment early next morning. She's wearing a nightgown and robe. She has a cup of coffee in her hand and she's talking to herself)

That's it. It's all so clear now. Ruthie told me what Jack said …and did…but he doesn't know it wasn't me. So all I have to do is pretend he was talking to me last night here and pick up from there. But, what am I going to tell him? I like him and may be even fond of him. But love? Besides, Ruthie didn't say anything about his proposing marriage, just going to Chicago. Does he mean my going to Chicago just to live with him? That's a giant step in our relationship. If I'm going to make a giant step with him, it's going to be the giant step to the altar. And, I'm not sure I want to make that step just yet.

But, no matter! The first step will be to sit down with him and let him know how I feel about his "proposal" that I never really got in the first place. Then, I can keep Ruthie out of this matter! It's confusing enough. But, that's what I'll do. I'll call and tell him I'll meet him tonight so we can clear the air.

(Goes to bedroom to dress as lights go down)

(Phone rings in Jack's apartment as he comes out of bedroom adjusting his tie, getting ready to go to work. He answers phone)

JACK: Hello! Oh, Pete! What brings you to call me so early in the morning. Oh! That's right, it's early afternoon in London. Why the call? Oh, you're in Heathrow getting ready to board a plane for New York right now. Well, great! As soon as you get to New York, call me and we can make arrangements to have you meet Holly…that's right, Holly, the girl I'm going out with. And marry? Oh, in time, in time. Hey! Have a good flight and call me when you get to New York.

(Hangs up and puts on his coat, opens his brief case to check papers.)

(Lights come up on Holly's apartment. She's fully dressed for work. She quickly picks up the phone and dials. The phone rings in Jack's apartment. He picks it up)

HOLLY: Hello, Jack!

JACK: Holly! What a wonderful surprise!

HOLLY: Jack, I've been thinking about our conversation last night. Oh, right, conversations. No matter! Why don't I come over to your place after work and we'll talk this out.

JACK: That'll be great. I can't wait. Couldn't we have dinner in a nice restaurant and talk there?

HOLLY: It would be better without the distraction of a restaurant.

JACK: Okay! You're right! Here will be fine. What time?

HOLLY: I'll see you about six o'clock. Good! *(Both hang up the phone. Jack snaps shut his brief case and exits his apartments as Holly dials her phone again.)* Ruthie! What's that noise! Oh, you're in a taxi on the way to an appointment. Okay, this'll be quick. I've decided to sit down with

Jack and tell him everything. Where? Oh, at his apartment. I don't want to meet him here with a picture in my mind of him proposing to you and kissing you. I need to straighten this out with a clear head. Help! No, I think you better stay out of this. I'll let you know how it turns out. Okay! I'll call you. *(Hangs up, checks the mirror and picks up her brief case)*. I don't know for sure what I'm going to say to him but I've got to say something that makes sense.

(Holly exits door)

(Early evening. Jack enters his apartment, drops his briefcase on table as phone rings.)

JACK: *(Picks up phone)* Hiya, Holly! Oh! It's you, Pete! Where are you? Just landed at Kennedy. That was fast! You had tailwinds! Good! I'm waiting for Holly to come over. I'm looking forward to getting our relationship settled. Yes, I'm really serious about this girl. Maybe next year! I don't want to rush into anything but I know I can't live in Chicago without her being with me. No! It's not selfish...That's great! You'll be here tomorrow. Good! I want you to meet Holly. Then you'll know why I want her to go to Chicago with me. I'll leave a key with the doorman so when you arrive in town you can come straight here. Wonderful! I'll see you tomorrow night!

(Jack takes off jacket, goes into bedroom. Comes back into living room as doorbell rings. He opens door and Holly is standing there.)

JACK: Holly! *(Embraces her, she dodges his kiss)* I'm so happy you decided to come over tonight. *(She puts her handbag on the phone table as she disengages herself from him)* Would you like a drink?

HOLLY: Yes! I better have one!

JACK: *(Making drinks at bar)* Holly! As I told you last night, I've got a great offer to join the home office in Chicago as vice-president for client relations.

HOLLY: I'm impressed. Congratulations!

JACK: I should be beside myself...

HOLLY: Yes! You should!

JACK: But, I can't consider taking the job unless you agree to go with me!

HOLLY: I don't understand you.

JACK: What don't you understand? I love you and want you with me…

HOLLY: When did love enter the picture?

JACK: As I told you last night, I've grown fond of you, enjoyed going out with you and grew to love you.

HOLLY: I had no idea. Look, Jack! We've gone to dinner, caught some shows, and gone to some weekend dances…but never once did I get the impression you had any real romantic feelings about me.

JACK: Haven't I kissed you goodnight after a night out to dinner or a show?

HOLLY: Yes, you have! But, I saw that in much the same manner as a handshake, just a little more intimate.

JACK: A handshake? A handshake? That's all they were to you. What about the other night when I first told you about my new job? Those kisses were no handshakes.

HOLLY: They weren't? Well, you must have been caught up in the moment and maybe I responded but that was merely an momentary emotion…I think!

JACK: Holly! I don't understand! I thought you saw our relationship growing into something more than friendship.

HOLLY: Like lovers? Hah! Why? I can't remember having to defend my virtue with you.

JACK: I respect you! I didn't want to make a wrong move.

HOLLY: Wrong move? How was I to know you were falling in love with me, as you say, if you didn't make some indication that you wanted our friendship to go further than dinner, shows and dancing?

JACK: Why? Would you feel better if I suggested we drive to a cheap motel or have you sleep over at my place some weekend?

HOLLY: Maybe not but at least I would have known that friendship had reached another plateau.

JACK: Would you have slept over? Or, gone on a weekend at some seaside resort?

HOLLY: I'm not saying I would…but then I'm not saying I wouldn't had I known we were on the same page.

JACK: But, Holly, I don't see you as a casual pickup, someone to discard after having a fling!

HOLLY: Well, Jack, I appreciate that but I don't know how you can expect me to be more than a good friend at a moment's notice. You say you want me to go to Chicago with you! Boy! That's certainly more than a weekend trip to the shore. What would going to Chicago mean? Moving in together?

JACK: It could! But, it would be your call.

HOLLY: My call? That's a big step, Jack! That's something that develops over months or even years, not when a big promotion stirs the fires. Frankly, a step like that has as much planning as a wedding does.

JACK: *(Thinks quickly)* Well, let's get married!

HOLLY: Married? Just like that! I guess I don't know you at all. I enjoyed going out with a man, secure in his profession, a fine conversationalist and a guy with a sense of humor…

JACK: Well, thank you for that but this is no joke!

HOLLY: No, it isn't! And, it's not something we can decide in a matter of days.

JACK: *(Crestfallen)* Well, I guess you're right!

HOLLY: Look, Jack! Let's sort of start over. My parents live in Chicago

JACK: *(Brightens)* They do!

HOLLY: Yes, and I visit them fairly often. So, we can e-mail each other or call each other by phone and then get together when I visit my folks.

JACK: It's not what I dreamed of.

HOLLY: Jack, I guess we weren't using the same sleeping pills.

JACK: *(Laughs)* I'll send you some of mine.

HOLLY: Gift wrapped? *(Laughs, then serious)* Let's take this slowly, all right? Jack, I am fond of you and certainly like to be with you. But, you have to know that this whole thing took me by surprise, to say the least

JACK: Everything this week took me by surprise...the job offer... my feelings for you! *(Moves to the door, opens it)* Here, let me take you home.

HOLLY: No, Jack! I have my car...and I do need to do a lot of thinking by myself. *(He nods his head, she moves to him, takes his head in her hands and kisses him, a little longer that just goodnight. He is pleasantly taken back)* Now, go take your sleeping pills. Goodnight. *(She exits as he turns towards audience with a look of hope as stage lights dim)*

End of Act One

"Double Trouble"
ACT TWO

(At opening of act, Holly is in her apartment on phone with Ruthie)

HOLLY: I'm telling you, Ruthie, everything is going to be all right. You didn't mess up my life. Jack and I met last night and we talked calmly about the situation and I think we have a solution that will satisfy both of us. We're going to take it slowly. He'll go to Chicago and I told him about my parents living there and....Yes, Ruthie, I know they're your parents too. That's not the point. I said I visit them occasionally and when I do, he and I can visit, go to dinner and see how the relationship develops. No, Ruthie, I didn't tell him that he was talking to you the other night. Maybe some time in the future we can deal with that. No! I'm not mad about the situation. Maybe in some strange way, your meeting him that way made it easier for me to deal with it. It gave me time to think over what he said to you thinking he was saying it to me. Yes, it really sounds confusing in the retelling. But, by all means, don't you try to explain the situation of the other night to him right now. Promise! I said: "Promise!"

Okay, that's a promise. I'll talk to you. *(Hangs up, Holly exits into bedroom)*

(Jack's apartment is dark as we hear key in front door and a man enters with the key that he puts in his pocket. He turns on the light and we see it's Jack...no it's Pete, who is Jack's twin brother, they look exactly alike.)

(He goes to phone, dials and then...)

PETE: Hello, Jack! The doorman gave me the key all right and I'm in your apartment. *(Looks around)* Not bad, not bad! Hey! I'm tired from the flight. Why don't you bring in something. Chinese! What a wonderful imagination you have. Never mind! Chinese sounds good to me after that long flight and a salad and a bag of peanuts. Okay! I'll make myself at home. See you later! *(Hangs up phone, looks at picture of woman, obviously Holly. He muses: "Hmmm! Jack's done alright for himself!" He replaces photo on table and looks around and goes to bedroom door, opens it and obviously sees the bathroom off stage. He enters)*

(There is a moment's delay and we hear the water flush and immediately afterwards, the doorbell rings. Pete enters from bedroom with a towel in his hands, his sleeves rolled up, as he is drying his hands. He goes to door and opens it and Holly steps into the room except it isn't Holly, it is Ruthie)

(Looking at picture, he speaks) Holly! This is a surprise!

RUTH: *(Raises her eyes as if saying: "Here we go again!)* Look, Jack! I've got to tell you something..

PETE: Well, first of all, Holly, you see I'm not...

RUTH: Look, the other night when you told me you loved me...

PETE: I did...! *(Really puzzled)*

RUTH: And, then when you kissed me...

PETE: I did?

RUTH: You know you did and I want to explain...

PETE: There's no explanations needed....I kissed you, huh!

RUTH: Com'on, Jack! Don't make this explanation any more difficult than it is.

PETE: *(Playing along)* No need explaining whatever it is!

RUTH: But, Jack! I've got to tell you the truth!

PETE: Well, if you insist!

RUTH: Jack! I'm not Holly!

PETE: You're not! *(Looks at photo on desk)* Of course, you are!

RUTH: No, Jack! I'm Holly's twin sister, Ruth!

PETE: *(Incredulous)* You're not Holly!

RUTH: Oh, Jack! I'm so sorry that it happened

PETE: *(Now speaking as Jack)* Well, nothing happened, really!

RUTH: Jack! Your confession of your love for Holly and your kissing me.

PETE: *(Tries to pass it off)* Well, that's okay! It was nothing.

RUTH: Nothing! Here I was making out with my sister's boyfriend.

PETE: *(Trying to figure out situation)* Well, no harm done.

RUTH: When I told Holly about it, she was very upset.

PETE: Oh! You told Holly about it!

RUTH: Yes, but she said she forgave me, but I wonder if she ever will. Will you tell her you made an innocent mistake. You thought I was she…Holly, that is.

PETE: You are a perfect double! *(Nothing to lose)* Sure, I'll explain it to her.

RUTH: Oh! Thanks! I'll never forget it. I want her to be happy and I don't want you to hate me for not telling you who I was.

PETE: Don't worry, I won't and I don't!

RUTH: Well, I feel better! Holly didn't want me to come over but I felt I had to clear my conscience.

PETE: Well, consider it cleared.

RUTH: Thank you! *(Starts to door)* This is just between us, all right?

PETE: Just between us of course! Wait! Do you have to leave? How about a drink to cement our agreement?

RUTH: I really shouldn't! Well, maybe one won't hurt.

PETE: Of course, it won't. After all, we may be in-laws someday!

RUTH: I hope so. Holly deserves a good man in her life.

PETE: Well, thank you! *(Hands her a drink)* Let's sit for a moment.

RUTH: *(She sits, then sips drink, after he clinks her glass with his)* Whew!! It's a relief to have you know the truth about me.

PETE: *(Moves closer to her, she doesn't move)* I'm pleased to meet Holly's sister. Just imagine! There's another woman as beautiful as Holly.

RUTH: You think Holly's beautiful?

PETE: Of course, she is! *(Puts arm around Ruth who takes no notice)* And, so are you.

RUTH: *(Coquettish)* You think so? I don't have too many men tell me that!

PETE: Well, there's something wrong with the men around here then! Any man in his right mind and with reasonable eyesight would think so…you're beautiful!

RUTH: *(Now comfortable as she sips her drink)* Thank you. Holly and I always had fun looking alike, especially in high school. But, as we got older, it became sort of double trouble. People began confusing us for each other and especially when we started working. It's one reason Holly came here while I stayed in Chicago. You'll like Chicago by the way.

PETE: I will?

RUTH: Yes! With your new job, you have to move to Chicago. Remember! That's what you told me when we first met the other night when you thought I was Holly.

PETE: *(Covers himself)* Of course! Chicago! You know, Ruth, you make a man forget everything when he's with you!

RUTH: Well, I don't know about that. I don't get too many chances to meet men for any length of time. I travel a lot in my job. I'm a convention planner operating out of Chicago but it takes me all over the country. So, I'm not in any one spot long enough to develop a relationship except an occasional dinner with a salesman or conventioneer. And they also have other ideas…like one-night stands.

PETE: The traveling salesman, huh! But don't blame them. Listen, you're a person who would make a man want to travel the world with you!

RUTH: I am? I'm surprised Holly hasn't accepted your proposal already with your line.

PETE: *(Freshens her drink)* You think it's a line!

RUTH: But, it's Holly you love! Right?

PETE: But, you make her so vivid in my mind it's as if she's right in front of me. *(Starts to embrace her)* It's just like being here with Holly.

RUTH: *(Sips drink)* But, I'm not Holly!

PETE: But, I can play make believe, can't I. *(Kisses her on the back of her neck)*

RUTH: What was that for?

PETE: *(Kisses her again)* It's all in the family, sort of!

RUTH: But, it's Holly you love....not me!

PETE: *(Stands, still embracing her as she rises)* You are very lovable, you know. I could believe you're Holly!

RUTH: *(Moves with him as he guides her towards the bedroom)* You think I am like her?

PETE: *(Now near the bedroom)* Of course, I do. Who wouldn't?

RUTH: *(Feeling her drinks)* I never really met a man like you!

PETE: *(Guides her into the bedroom as he responds)* You've must have had many men wanting to be with you.

RUTH: *(Now entering bedroom, still in his arms)* Not r-e-a-l-l-y!!!! *(They disappear in the bedroom)* Don't Jack! You'll tear my blouse! Wait! I'll get it.

PETE: *(From bedroom)* Oh! Holly! I can't wait to make love to you!

RUTH: Jack! I'm Ruth, don't you remember! Don't break the zipper!

PETE: We can't lose this moment!

(There's a noise of a key in the apartment door)

RUTH: *(She rushes into main room, zipping up her skirt with blouse open, looks back at bedroom)* I'm sorry, Jack! I just can't do this to Holly!

PETE: *(Still from bedroom)* But, you're Holly to me

RUTH: *(Starts buttoning her blouse, as apartment door opens, Jack appears, Ruth is aghast)* Jack! How did you get out into the hall?

JACK: Holly! How did you get here!

RUTH: I came to apologize! Wait a minute!… I'm not Holly!

JACK: You're not!

RUTH: I'm Holly's sister, her twin sister!

JACK: Twin sister?????

RUTH: Yes! And, how did you get out in the hall. You were just in the bedroom!

JACK: The bedroom? *(He rushes to the bedroom, goes in and says)* Pete!!! What are you doing in bed? And what were you doing with Holly?

RUTH: I'm not Holly!! And who's that in the bedroom????

JACK: It's Pete!! My brother..my twin brother!!!

RUTH: Your twin brother? He's not Jack!!!

JACK: No! I'm Jack! Didn't he introduce himself to you!

RUTH: No! He kept calling me Holly, even when I told him I was Ruth!!!

JACK: *(Back at the bedroom door)* Pete! Put your clothes on so I can throw you out bodily

RUTH: Oh! Don't hurt him!!

JACK: Hurt him!!! I could kill him only they'd probably bury me.

RUTH: He didn't do anything! Honest!!!

JACK: He didn't do anything? He knew you weren't Holly while you thought he was me...Jack!

RUTH: *(Thinks a second)* Yes!!!

JACK. And, he was making it look like I m trying to take Holly's sister to bed…

RUTH: He was very persuasive…but I wasn't really going to do anything.

JACK: You were willing to make love to your sister's boyfriend!

RUTH: But, he's not Holly's boyfriend!

JACK: But, you didn't know that when you followed him into that room! *(Points to the bedroom)*

RUTH: But, we didn't do anything…honest! You see, I'm still dressed. I was getting ready to leave when you came in

JACK: How are we going to explain this to Holly!!

RUTH: Explain it to Holly? We don't have to! Nothing happened!

JACK: It could have!

RUTH: *(Emphatically)* But, it didn't!

PETE: *(From offstage, stage manager as Pete)* Nothing happened!!

JACK: Never mind, you!!! I'll deal with you later.

RUTH: *(Has fixed her hair and moves to the apartment door to exit)* I better go, I don't want to be in the middle of a brothers' fight. I've had enough excitement for today…or a lifetime.

JACK: *(Opens door for her)* Not a word to Holly, you understand!

RUTH: I may be insane…but I'm not crazy. *(Exits)*

JACK: *(Closes door and makes his way towards bedroom door)* Okay!! Now, let's hear your side of the story!!! *(Exits into bedroom as lights dim)*

(Lights come up on Holly's apartment, Holly enters, puts down bags and answers ringing phone)

HOLLY: Ruthie! Are you all right? You sound excited! Okay! You're not excited. What! You have to go back to Chicago? Why? I thought you were going to be here for the whole week. Oh! Something came up at the main office that needs your help. But, I wanted you to meet Jack the right way. What? You don't think you could face him again! But, you can't just ignore him. After all, he and I may wind up being more than friends at some point in the future. What? Does Jack have any relatives that he's talked about? Come to think of it, he hasn't. At least no one he mentioned. It'd be what? Oh! If he had a brother like himself, we could double date! Even if he had, let's wait until my relationship gets better organized. Double date! We'd only wind up with the same problem we had with boys in high school and just this week with Jack. Too much confusion! We better do separate dating. What? You want to be maid of honor at my wedding? Who's talking about weddings? Well, maybe if things go along well.

(Light goes down on Holly's apartment but Holly stays on phone)

(Light comes up at Jack's apartment. Jack answers phone. It's Pete apologizing.)

JACK: Pete! Never mind apologizing. You're a womanizer, you've always been. Listen, you've got me in plenty of trouble over the years. I've had my face slapped by more girls because of what you said to them. Never mind we could have had a lot of fun! I didn't want to fool them into thinking we were each other. Look! I'm going over to Holly's now and try to straighten this all out. Yes! I'm going to tell her the truth about you and her sister. She might as well know that her sister made a play for me even though it wasn't me. Well, apologize to her all you want.

(Hangs up phone. Light goes down on Jack's apartment, comes up on Holly's)

HOLLY: *(Holly on phone with Ruth)*….Okay, Ruthie! If you have to go, you have to go. Give my best to mom and dad. Tell them, I'll call. *(Holly hangs up. After an interval, the doorbell rings. Holly opens door and it's Jack!)* Jack! This is a surprise.

JACK: I had to come over and apologize all over again!

HOLLY: For what!

JACK: For my brother!

HOLLY: You have a brother!

JACK: Yes! I have a brother! He visited me tonight!

HOLLY: So?

JACK: Pete is my twin brother!

HOLLY: You have a twin brother?

JACK: Yes! And, we look exactly alike!

HOLLY: Tell me I haven't met him when I thought I was meeting you!

JACK: No, you haven't met him but your sister has!

HOLLY: He met my sister! Where?

JACK: In my apartment!

HOLLY: In your apartment! What was she doing there?

JACK: Apparently, she was trying to apologize to me for our misunderstanding several days ago!

HOLLY: I told her to leave apologizing alone!

JACK: Well, apparently, she didn't listen to you. And, to compound it, Pete went along with her and pretended to be me.

HOLLY: And, she believed he was you?

JACK: Pete doesn't miss a beat. They apparently had a few drinks and he was luring her into my bedroom when I arrived home.

HOLLY: She thought your brother was you and she was going to bed with him.

JACK: He's very persuasive! And, she did have a few drinks!

HOLLY: How could she?

JACK: I'm sure she didn't mean to hurt you!

HOLLY: First you think my sister is me and you pour out your soul to her and she doesn't explain who she is…and now, your brother makes believe he's you so he can take my sister to…Oh! I'm all mixed up now.

JACK: I'm sorry! I didn't want to upset you. But, I thought we ought to try to get this straightened out before it got completely out of control.

HOLLY: Jack! You're right! Maybe we better get this straightened out, if we are going to have any sort of real relationship.

JACK: Yes! I do want a real relationship! *(He embraces her and she responds)*

HOLLY: *(Breaks the embrace)* Maybe we ought to go out to dinner and talk it out without letting our emotions get the better of us. *(They exit, Holly first, Jack next and he closes the door. The lights in her apartment dim out.)*

(After a short interval. Pete comes out of Jack's bedroom with his cell phone.)

PETE: This is Pete! Look, Ruth! I'm serious. I am sorry about the other night. Yes, I will apologize to your sister. It was just a natural instinct with me. I always used my brother's likeness to me to try to steal his girlfriends. Why, he was getting Valentine's cards from girls he never met. No! It's really not a game with me…well, maybe it is sometimes. Look, I have to admit, I was taken with you the other night…yes, I know I really thought you were Holly. No! I don't always try to make love to my brother's girl friends…well, not too often! Hey! Don't get high and mighty! Didn't you think you were being seduced by my brother Jack, your sister's boyfriend, and you were going along with it. Oh! You're sorry about that..it was the drinks!

Well, no matter! I apologize because it looks like my brother is serious about your sister and I don't want to cause hard feelings. Oh! You don't either. Well, we have something in common there. How did I get your phone number? I had your name and I knew you were staying at a local hotel, so I called around until you answered. Look! Why don't we have dinner I'll pick you up and we can get to know each other the right way... at a great place I know in town with good food, great drinks, old movies and dancing. What? Don't worry, you'll understand when you see it. Good! I'll pick you up in a half hour! *(He hangs up phone)* Here we go again! *(Opens door and leaves, as lights come down in Jack's apartment)*

(Lights come up in Holly's apartment as door opens and Holly enters with Jack holding her hand)

HOLLY: Jack! That was fun! All the time I've been in town, I never knew that French restaurant existed.

JACK: That was my closer! I saved that for the right time.

HOLLY: The right time?

JACK: Yes! When I felt we had gone past being friends.

HOLLY: Gone past being friends?

JACK: Yes! *(Embraces her)* Will you believe me when I tell you I love you?

HOLLY: Should I?

JACK: Yes! *(Kisses her)* I love you!

HOLLY: *(Returns his kiss, then laughs gently)* And, I love you!

JACK: Well, where does that leave us?

HOLLY: I suppose I could move back to Chicago and work from there.

JACK: Yes! And, we could be together....

HOLLY: In my own apartment!

JACK: *(Smiles)* Not in your family's house?

HOLLY: *(Emphatic)* In my own apartment!

JACK: You can live in Chicago and still work on your dress designs?

HOLLY: I could design in a phone booth as long as there are planes to take me to the manufacturers of the dresses I design.

(Jack embraces her, she responds as she leads him to the door) Now, you better go before we....before we forget our good intentions to play it fair and square!

JACK: We'll play it slow...I promise! But, you're going to know I love you! *(They are at the door, he kisses her. She opens door)*

HOLLY: Thanks for a lovely evening! And, for a lovely future...

JACK: That I promise! *(He leaves, and Holly closes the door, leans against it, closes her eyes and smiles. Then, she moves towards bedroom door as lights dim)*

(After an interval, laughter is heard outside Jack's apartment, the door opens and Ruth walks in a little unsteadily and Pete follows, locks the door and embraces her. She responds and then walks about the room)

RUTH: *(Haltingly)* I never knew you liked old movies!

PETE: *(Smugly)* Of course! They're so corny, like Gable's "Frankly, my dear, I don't give a damn!"

RUTH: "I vant to be alone!"

PETE: Yeah! Garbo!

RUTH: Right!

PETE: And, where else can you find big screen movies in a bar...and with dancing!

RUTH: I haven't danced so much since I was in college! *(Whirls about and almost loses her footing)*

PETE: How about a nightcap? *(He turns toward table with liquor bottles and begins pouring two glasses)*

(Turns around and Ruth is gone, then he hears her voice from the bedroom)

RUTH: *(Offstage)* "I'm ready for my close up, Mr. DeMille! *(Laughs)*

PETE: *(Laughs as he crosses to bedroom)* All right, Miss Swanson! Lights! Camera! Action! *(enters bedroom as lights start to dim out)*

RUTH: *(Offstage)* Oh, yes! Oh, yes! Ooooooooooooh, Cecil! Yes!.... Yes!...... Yessssssss!

(LIGHTS OUT)

END OF PLAY

"Chat Room"

A New Comedy

By Martin P. Kelly

Note from the Author

This play was written at first as an exercise in constructing the possibility of two middle-aged people finding each other on an Internet "chat room." There they "talk" to each other over weeks and months only to find that they had developed an affection for each other even though they've never really met.

When I began to think of them as friends, I kept working on the play until I found the end that was satisfying for me, the characters and hopefully, for an audience.

MPK

"Chat Room"
ACT ONE

(At curtain rise, the audience sees two rooms in separate apartments, one lived in by Eddie Cloran. It's a disheveled place with a laptop computer on a small desk facing the audience. The other apartment is neat and sparsely decorated in which Norah Phillips lives. Norah also has a laptop computer. Eddie is a widower of five years while Norah is a divorcee for at least four years. He is in his early-60s, she in her late 50s. Both computer monitors are pointed upstage so the audience can't see them. Norah is on the phone with a friend.)

NORAH: *(Into phone)* Of course, I didn't tell him the truth. What am I going to do Sally, tell him I'm in my 50s, divorced for four years from a guy who ran away with his blonde paralegal? ... Yeah! Yeah! I know! Honesty is the best policy! That's before they had chat rooms. Now, we bend the truth and let things fall where they may.

I gotta go! Ronnie gets into the chat room early. Did I give him my real name? Of course not! He thinks I'm Daphne and 39 years old with a great body! I'll talk to you in the morning. Goodnight! *(She hangs up and leaves the room, talking to herself)* If I don't get to the john, I'll never last two minutes on the computer.

(Eddie enters his room, carrying a sandwich and a bottle of beer. He sits at the computer and boots it up He is balding, paunchy but has a face that carries a lifetime of smiles on it.)

EDDIE: Let's see what my girl Daphne has to say tonight! *(He strokes message.)* Doesn't look like she's on the net yet! *(He takes a drink from the bottle, answers the phone as Norah enters her room and goes to the computer.)*

EDDIE: *(Into phone)* Yeah! This is Eddie! Your father! Who did I sound like, somebody else? Just call me Dad and I'll answer you with my real voice. Look, Teddy, you're my son and I love you dearly but you'd do better to remember what my voice sounds like. Your

69

kids better remember my voice when they call, if they call. Sure, sure! They're great kids and you have a great wife. Look! I'm busy now. Can I call you later? Give my best to the kids! Yes, yes! I have work to do on my computer...Oh, yeah! Thanks for the computer. *(He hangs up as Norah sits at the computer and strokes some keys.)*

NORAH: *(types)* Ronnie! This is Daphne! Are you there!

EDDIE: *(types)* Of course, I'm here, my love. Where else would I be?

NORAH: Did you miss me?

EDDIE: You bet I did! I even dreamed about you last night.

NORAH: You did?

EDDIE: Of course I did.

NORAH: What were we doing?

EDDIE: You'd never guess!

NORAH: Try me!

EDDIE: Alright, what do you think we were dong?

NORAH: Would I be presumptuous to hope we were getting sweaty!

EDDIE: No, you wouldn't. I know I was!

NORAH: Then I had to be reciprocating.

EDDIE: Yes, you were!

NORAH: I sure hope so!

EDDIE: Was it good for you?

NORAH: You ought to know. It was your dream!

EDDIE: You loved it! Hey! For a couple of 40 year olds, we better be good. In our prime and all that!

NORAH: Wait a minute! I'm 39! Remember?

EDDIE: So I'm 40 and took advantage of a younger woman.

NORAH: Please do! Now, I know why the people at work said I had a glow on by face today.

EDDIE: Then, you must have dreamed the same thing!

NORAH: Can't I dream, too?

EDDIE: Please! Be my guest!

NORAH: I will but I better cool down. Whew! So! How was your job today?

EDDIE: Same as always! Listen! The five guys working for me couldn't sell bottled water in a desert. I have to do all the follow ups and keep after them all the time.

NORAH: I know the feeling! The clerks I have at this office are the laziest bunch you'd ever see. They don't know the meaning of work.

EDDIE: Why don't you fire them?

NORAH: Hey! It takes an act of Congress to let civil servants go. Didn't you know that?

EDDIE: It's a good thing I'm not in government work. Listen, I fired two guys a couple of weeks ago. They don't produce out they go!

NORAH: Well, aren't you a man of action!

EDDIE: Believe me, you can't let them get to you. No production, no job! That's all there is to it.

NORAH: You sound so decisive. I wish I could do that.

EDDIE: Don't let them grind you down, that's all.

NORAH: I'll remember that!

EDDIE: Hey, let's not talk shop. Did you think of me today?

NORAH: Of course I did. Why wouldn't I after last night, in our dreams.

EDDIE: I couldn't get you out of my mind all day. You know, there were times I was almost nice to the clowns at the office!

NORAH: How long has it been since we first met? A month!

EDDIE: We met right here twenty-nine days ago!

NORAH: You know exactly?

EDDIE: I have a note here on the computer. It's the day and the hour I first ran across your message.

NORAH: I almost didn't write that message.

EDDIE: *"Anybody out there interesting enough to talk to me?"* That was your message. It was so impertinent that I couldn't resist answering you.

NORAH: You were the fourth person who did.

EDDIE: That's what you told me. I appreciated your candor.

NORAH: There were two other guys who wanted to talk about sex right away and a woman trying to sell me insurance.

EDDIE: I'm glad I made the cut.

NORAH: Are you, really?

EDDIE: Hey, I've been here 29 straight nights, right?

NORAH: Yes, you have and I've looked forward to every night we've chatted.

EDDIE: You know, I don't understand why you need to meet a man on a chat room? After all, you're 5'9, long blonde hair, slim figure. Did I get that message right?

NORAH: Right on the button!

EDDIE: Well, why a chat room?

NORAH: I could ask you the same thing.

EDDIE: You could, but I asked you first.

NORAH: Well, I'm not a drinker and I don't like bars. I'm not overly religious, so the church socials are out. I have trouble talking to people.

EDDIE: You don't have trouble talking to me!

NORAH: It's different. I could always write letters easily and express my feelings in them but, in person, I'm a total flop.

EDDIE: I doubt that!

NORAH: No, really! I have trouble meeting people, talking to them.

EDDIE: A 5-9 blonde with a slim figure doesn't have to do much talking.

NORAH: You know what I mean! Men I've met see only the outer me, the blonde, slim woman and that's all they want. If that's all I wanted, I could be spending all my time on a Sealy!

EDDIE: Now, that's an image!

NORAH: File it in your dreams. But what about you and women?

EDDIE: It's strange! There's a parallel. Women I've met see me only as the tall guy with wavy hair who wears clothes well. They are disappointed if I don't make a pass at them the first couple of minutes of conversation.

NORAH: Is that bad? I'd think a man would be flattered to be wanted by women right away!

EDDIE: Sure, it's flattering to a point but I like the company of women, to talk to them, to make them laugh, especially after trying to make the jokers at work do a day's work. I don't really see myself as a guy flitting about from bed to bed with willing women.

NORAH: Well, that's comforting, I think! What about your dream last night?

EDDIE: Well, that's the point! It was a dream and I could be perfect and you could be perfect, at least in my concept of perfect. And, we can still be friends and to talk as we do.

NORAH: Couldn't we be friends if we met in person?

EDDIE: I would hope so but I can't be sure that it would be the same.

NORAH: I think I understand! It's the same with me. We're both young enough to be full of life and yet we seem bound to meet this way and find a friendship that's complete in some form.

EDDIE: At this point, I'm satisfied.

NORAH: Well, don't get too satisfied. You never know where this will lead.

EDDIE: I'm willing to follow wherever it goes!

NORAH: Well, travel on! By the way, have you done much traveling?

EDDIE: Not in the last five years! But, before that, I did some. There was this woman I went on a cruise with...

NORAH: Now, I'm jealous... a cruise, you say?

EDDIE: Yeah! We hit some spots in the Caribbean, including Jamaica. We walked up a waterfall..

NORAH: You what!

EDDIE: Oh, it's a tourist thing. There's a waterfall, that comes down gradually over a long area and you walk up on a series of flat stones. It was fun, holding her hand as she gasped at the thrill of it, walking barefoot up the smooth stones.

NORAH: And, you made it all the way up.

EDDIE: Oh, yes! It's about six stories high but it's a gradual climb.

NORAH: It all sounds romantic. I'm jealous!

EDDIE: I don't mean to make you jealous.

NORAH: Tell me more!

EDDIE: Well, it was romantic, as you say. And, later we went to a market where Beatrice bought...

NORAH: Her name was Beatrice?

EDDIE: Yes, everybody called her Bea, but I liked her full name, Beatrice!

NORAH: So, what happened at the market?

EDDIE: She bought a straw basket and almost started a riot. Every native vendor followed us down the street, offering her baskets of all types for bargain prices. I think she bought a dozen more before I could get her out of the crowd.

NORAH: She sounds like quite a wonderful woman.

EDDIE: She was!

NORAH: The experience sounded like fun!

EDDIE: It was hectic but it's a good memory.

NORAH: What happened to Beatrice?

EDDIE: We parted!

NORAH: Oh! Did you have a fight?

EDDIE: No. *(Beat)* She passed away...a heart attack!

NORAH: Oh, my God! And so young!

EDDIE: Yes! She was young...young in every way!

NORAH: I'm so sorry!

EDDIE: Thank you!

NORAH: You are fortunate to have that memory.

EDDIE: Yes, I am! What about you! Did you have someone?

NORAH: Certainly nothing like you! There were a few guys but only one serious. I met him in Central Park. He was feeding squirrels. That should have tipped me off.

EDDIE: It went bad, I take it?

NORAH: Not at first! He had a charm about him but he was a gambler and started to borrow money. That should have been a tip off! But, it wasn't so obvious at first, until he had borrowed $5,000 from me and then left with a redhead. I think she was a dental hygienist.

EDDIE: A dental hygienist!

NORAH: That's right! What could she have found so attractive about an open mouth?

EDDIE: I couldn't tell you!

NORAH: Well, he'll always have clean teeth!

EDDIE: There's a reason to run off with her!

NORAH: I hope they all fall out! The teeth, that is!

EDDIE: I'm sorry! Hey, let's forget him and think of us! Okay?

NORAH: You're right! Let's think about us tonight!

EDDIE: You going to dream of me again?

NORAH: I will, if you will.

EDDIE: I promise and how!

NORAH: Good! *(Phone rings in Norah's apartment)*

NORAH: Let me sign off. My phone's ringing!

EDDIE: I have to make a call, too! I'll talk to you tomorrow night.

NORAH: I can't wait!

EDDIE: Goodnight!

NORAH: Goodnight!

(She clicks off computer, as does Eddie who leaves his room, as Norah picks up ringing phone)

NORAH: Yes, Sally! How did I know it was you? I have caller ID, remember? That's right. I was talking to Ronnie. Yes, it was a good conversation! No, he didn't talk dirty! Who the hell do you think I am? I'm not going to talk to a guy who talks dirty. He did say, he dreamed of me last night. Never mind what he dreamed. He also told me of a girlfriend he had. She died though. Yeah! Five years ago. I think he was in love with her. No! I haven't told him the truth about my age. What do you think I want to do, chase him away. Besides, this is the age for older women to be with younger men!

Remember? I don't expect to ever meet him, so why tell the truth. It's more fun this way and I sort of like what he sounds like. Yeah! See you at work tomorrow! Some day I hope I can get out of sorting the books in the basement. Yeah! It's a job and you can't be choosy when you're 59, no pension and waiting for Social Security to kick in.

(She hangs up phone and leaves her room as Eddie comes into his room, picks up phone and dials.)

EDDIE: It's me, Eddie! Oh, you recognize my voice now! Has she gone to sleep yet! Good! Let me say good night to her.*(Fiddles with playing cards)* Hello, Little Bea. You sleepy yet! You are! Good! I just wanted to say goodnight. Did your father read you a story? He did! Good! *(To himself)* It's nice to have a son who can read. *(Back to phone)* No! I was just talking to myself. You're what? Oh! You're going to be four years old next week? Well now, I think you're right! What would you like for your birthday? You want a new name? Why? You don't like Bea? But that's just a shorter version of Beatrice. That was your grandmother's name. Your father and mother wanted to keep her memory alive by naming you after your grandmother. Yes, dear! She was my wife. Where is she? She's in heaven. She went there a few weeks before you were born. You kinda changed places. So, they thought they'd name you after her. Do you understand? No! I guess that's a little confusing. But, some day you'll understand and you'll realize it's a nice name. Remind me to tell you about a trip to Jamaica. No, not now! Maybe for your birthday! Do I what? Oh, yes! I miss her. Good night, honey. *(Hangs up phone, looks at nearby picture)* Yes! I miss you!

(Stage goes dark for a few moments, then lights come back on again)

(It is 8 p.m. the next night. Eddie enters room carrying a box of cookies. Picks up phone)

EDDIE: *(mumbles into phone)* Hemmo!! Nomph, id's me *(Clears throat)*, Me, your father. What do you mean you couldn't understand me? It's those cookies your wife sent me. They're great but chewy and I had one in my mouth when I called. I'm sorry I was eating a cookie when I dialed. Big deal! Yeah! I love you too. Let me talk to Marge. Marge, your wife! The cookie maker! *(To himself)* Where the hell did he come from? *(Back to phone)* Oh! Marge. Just wanted to thank you for the cookies! *(Surprise!)* They're diet cookies! Really! You think I need diet cookies? Oh, it can't hurt. Do the two boys eat them? Not really! Okay! Thank you anyway. Can I say hello to Little Bea.? She's out with your mother. That's good! Remember now, I'd like to take her out sometime. Good! Thanks again for the diet cookies!

(Hangs up) Diet cookies! They'll drive the kids to fast food in a hurry! *(Pushes box of cookies away. Straightens up and pulls in stomach)* Next thing, she'll have me eating yogurt pie! *(Picks up box of cookies, exits to kitchen)*

(Norah enters, hair in rollers after shower and shampoo. Her phone rings)

NORAH: *(Picks up phone)* I'm sorry I didn't get back to you, Sally! Yes, I got your message. You want to see the latest disaster movie. Why? Just to see a lot of big, good-looking guys sweat. Join a gym! It won't be that more expensive and it's healthier. Oh! You don't want to smell sweat, just see it. Let's go see the latest Julia Roberts movie! I don't want to dream of monsters. Okay! Call me when you decide! *(Hangs up)* Why does she have to mention sweat after I've just showered?

(Checks computer, boots it up and does a few key strokes)

(Eddie comes out of kitchen with bag of potato chips, sits at computer)

EDDIE: Oh, Daphne's on! *(Sits, and does some key strokes)* Hello, again, girl of my dreams.

NORAH: Never mind! Last night was my night to dream! I kept thinking of that story about the waterfall you told me about last night. I had to go to the John at least three times. Oops! I shouldn't tell you things like that!

EDDIE: Hey, honey! What's normal, is normal! I do a bit of traveling myself at night but no matter. Was that all you dreamed about, a waterfall?

NORAH: Actually, it turned out to be very nice after awhile.

EDDIE: How nice?

NORAH: There was this water falling about six stories above and we were standing in the pool where it fell and we were behind the falls. You know like in the travel folders!

EDDIE: Did we have clothes on?

NORAH: Of course we did! But we weren't very dry!

EDDIE: Sort of an elaborate wet t-shirt event!

NORAH: You could say that, I guess!

EDDIE: Okay! I'll say it. Did we ever get out of the shower?

NORAH: Yes! We walked through the falls in the shallow pool to the shore and stretched out to dry off.

EDDIE: To dry off!

NORAH: Yes, dry off!

EDDIE: And, that's all?

NORAH: Well, we started to... .and then my bladder responded.

EDDIE: For a 39-nine year old willowy blonde, you have active waterworks.

NORAH: It's the birth control pills. That's how they affect me.

EDDIE: Didn't know you were on birth control pills.

NORAH: *(Laughs)* Never know when I'll get lucky.

EDDIE: Lucky? How the hell are you going to get lucky over the Internet? Or don't I know about transmitting something?

NORAH: I'm joking! Don't you know that?

EDDIE: Well, there are jokes and there are jokes.

NORAH: I'm sorry! Don't be petulant!

EDDIE: Well, suppose I talked about Viagra!

NORAH: I wouldn't think you would. A man like you, I would imagine you wouldn't need Viagra unless you plan to service the whole neighborhood. You're not planning to do that, are you?

EDDIE: Hardly! That doesn't sound right, does it? No, I'm having enough trouble dealing with one woman in a chat room.

NORAH: You think I'm difficult, do you?

EDDIE: You're intriguing and I am captivated by you. How do you like that? Captivated!

NORAH: I never thought of myself as captivating but if you think so, I'll be happy to accept the compliment.

EDDIE: Okay, then! You're captivating.

NORAH: That ought to set the dream going tonight!

EDDIE: Stay out of the waterfalls. I can't swim!

NORAH: Really, now! Promise me you'll think of me in your dreams.

EDDIE: I have a special sleeping pill for that...the "Daphne dream pill"!

NORAH: Take two... double your pleasure!

EDDIE: You got it! Good night!

NORAH: Good night...my sweet!

EDDIE: My sweet?

NORAH: Never mind, now, goodnight.

EDDIE: Goodnight, dream girl!

(Norah leaves room, rubbing the towel over her hair, Eddie picks up phone and dials...speaks with emphasis in the manner of a radio announcer.)

EDDIE: This...is...your...father. Listen, no cookies. I'm not being foolish. If I am, remember you're in the gene pool so you could be foolish, too! Okay! You went to college. So what! You can be just as foolish as guys like me. And, don't forget who sent you to college. You got an education, had your "foolish" gene altered and met the cookie mistress. You owe me for having to manage that roofing business all those years. Those five roofers drove me crazy. Never could keep up with them. Sometimes, they wouldn't answer their beepers for hours. Complaining! Who's complaining? Aw! Forget about it! Let me talk to Little Bea! No, I won't fill her head with foolishness... Hello, Little Bea! How are you today! Tired? Why? Mommy took you to the zoo. That's wonderful. What was your favorite animal? The elephants. Elephants, huh! Do you know why the elephants are called "tourists"? No? Because they're always carrying their trunks with them! Yeah! That's funny, isn't it? Don't forget to tell your Daddy that story. Alright! You get some sleep too, Goodnight, honey!

(Hangs up. Walks out of room)

Wait until the college graduate hears that! *(Laughs as he exits the room)*

(BLACKOUT)

(Next night. Norah is carrying a sandwich and a cup of coffee on a tray to the computer. The phone rings.)

NORAH: Oh, it's you, Sally! No, I was expecting you to call. Of course, it wouldn't be Ronnie. He doesn't have my phone number.

No, I don't think I'd give it to him, even if he asked. This is fun, at least for now I think about him at the library and it makes what I'm doing less tedious. Am I sorry I lied about my age and looks? What choice did I have? After all, he's only 40. I've had my fill of 40 year-old's, like the guy I married. Twenty years together and he runs off with his paralegal and leaves me flat. The alimony barely pays the rent and him a lawyer bilking seniors now in Florida. I hope an alligator bites him in the....what chance would I have, if Ronnie and I were to meet? That's easy for you to say. You try carrying on a romance in a chat room! You can't operate a computer! Good for you! No, I'm sure I wouldn't want to meet him in person.

(Eddie comes into his room, wiping his mouth with a napkin. He turns on the computer and enters a few key strokes.as his phone rings)

EDDIE: *(Answers phone)* Oh! It's you, issue of my loins!.. Well, I think it's funny!... You didn't like the elephant joke, either. Hey! I'll bet Little Bea told it to all her day care playmates. and they laughed. So there! Let's see, you called. What can I do for you? Did I what? Oh! My doctor's appointment tomorrow? I can't make it! Because I'm going to have something to do... What? I don't know yet but I'll think of something. Quit bugging me! Okay, I'll go to the doctor... Yeah! Yeah! He's the best one around. Thanks for nothing! I'll call you and let you know! Is Little Bea around! Oh, she's in bed already. No! The elephant joke didn't tire her out. Goodnight! *(Hangs up phone, starts for bedroom.)* Damn doctor! All he'll do is charge me $100 and then stick his finger up my...*(out of room)*

(Phone rings in Norah's apartment. Norah enters, carrying bag of groceries, puts them down near computer.)

NORAH: *(To phone)* Wait a minute! Wait a minute! Can't you see I'm busy. *(Puts down bags of groceries, picks up phone and is brusque)* Yes! What is it? Oh! It's you Sally. I'm sorry about being snappy to you. I've been busy shopping for groceries. Yes! I do cook for myself. Ronnie? Well, I can't feed him over the Internet. No! He hasn't asked me out! You ask far too many questions, you know that! Yes! I expect to talk to him tonight. Talk to you in the morning. *(Hangs up phone, turns to computer and boots it up, sits in front of it and types)*

Are you there, Ronnie? Hey! I'm talking to you.

(Eddie comes into room and c hecks computer)

EDDIE: There she is, just like clockwork! *(Sits at computer, types)* Hello, love of my life!

NORAH: Oh, I'm that, am I?

EDDIE: Only if you want to be!

NORAH: I do!

EDDIE: Tell me there's no minister standing next to you!

NORAH: What! Oh! No, there's no minister standing here or a justice of the peace, either.

EDDIE: I'd at least want a pre-nup first!

NORAH: You're getting ahead of yourself, aren't you?

EDDIE: Just playing the game, that's all!

NORAH: Well, some things aren't games, you know!

EDDIE: Okay, don't get all serious on me.

NORAH: How was your day?

EDDIE: Not much different from yesterday, except that crew of mine is just as dumb as they'll be next week, too.

NORAH: You have a tough life! That's what you get for being a boss.

EDDIE: It's tough being at the top, I can tell you!

NORAH: You sound a little testy tonight. What bit you?

EDDIE: Nothing bit me. It's just that a friend called to remind me I have a doctor's appointment tomorrow.

NORAH: Oh! Is it something that concerns you?

EDDIE: No! No! It's just a routine test. Tomorrow morning! The doctor just wants to put his finger on my health condition.

NORAH: What condition?

EDDIE: No condition! It's strictly routine.

NORAH: It better be! I can't afford to have a friend disappear on me.

EDDIE: You'd have no trouble making friends.

NORAH: I'd rather not think about it. Have any dreams lately?

EDDIE: Yeah! I was on a desert island with six beautiful women... one for love-making every day of the week with some rest on Sunday.

NORAH: *(Derisively)* In your dreams!!

EDDIE: That's what I said. It was a dream!

NORAH: So, what happened?

EDDIE: After several years of making love to six women every week with only Sunday to rest, out of the waves one day comes two blonde twin girls in bikinis.

NORAH: Yes!

EDDIE: And, they say: "What a perfectly delightful little island!"

NORAH: And what did you say?

EDDIE: "There go my Sundays!"

NORAH: You're ridiculous!!!!

EDDIE: Hey! You wanted a dream, so I gave you a story. It could have been a dream!

NORAH: I only want dreams with me in them.

EDDIE: You're pretty selfish, aren't you!

NORAH: I aim to be.

EDDIE: But, those girls deserve some fun too!

NORAH: Let them find their own chat room.

EDDIE: Okay! No more desert island dreams, unless you're on the island.

NORAH: Good! That's settled. Now, I'm going to bed and dream.

EDDIE: Don't leave me out!

NORAH: We'll see, we'll see! Goodnight!

EDDIE: Goodnight! *(Norah rises, and crosses out of room, muttering to herself.)*

NORAH: There go my Sundays...Hummph!

(BLACKOUT)

(It is next night Eddie is on the phone with his son.)

EDDIE: Don't tell your missus. It's probably nothing. Because I said it's probably nothing. And, don't go calling the doctor, just because you went to college with him. There's such a thing as patient confidentiality. What do you mean, "not when the patient is my father?" Stay out of this, will you? I'll handle it myself. And, don't go saying anything in front of Little Bea or the boys! It was only a biopsy. He didn't use a finger, this time. A needle, that's right! But, I didn't feel a thing, except embarrassment with his red-haired nurse helping him. Listen, if a redhead is going to see me that way, I don't want anyone else in the room. Don't you call me a dirty old man, I'm your father! Give me a little respect! Ha-ha! "You're giving me as little as possible." Very funny! Okay! I'll keep you informed. Goodnight. Kiss Little Bea for me.

(Hangs up, sits at the computer, turns it on but doesn't keystroke)

(Norah enters her room, with a salad plate in her hand, nibbling on it with a fork. She sits at the computer, turns it on, but doesn't key stroke it)

NORAH: *(To herself)* I wonder how Ronnie made out at the doctor's today? He was being too blase about it, I think.

EDDIE: *(To himself)* Let's see! Maybe if I just not even mention the test at all, I don't have to talk to her about it. That's it! I won't mention it.

(Norah starts typing)

NORAH: Hey, stranger! Are you ridin' the range tonight?

EDDIE: *(Types)* Yup! I'm sitting here in the saddle, ma'm, minding all the doggies.

NORAH: You'd make a lousy John Wayne with that dialogue.

EDDIE: Did John Wayne have dialogue?

NORAH: Never mind! Okay! How 'd you do today?

EDDIE: How did I do what today?

NORAH: The test, the test! How did you make out on the test!

EDDIE: Great! In fact, the doctor liked it so much he wanted to do another. So, I said: "Sure, go ahead!" And, he did.

NORAH: And, what's the test for!

EDDIE: I'm not sure! I couldn't see what he was doing. The redhead would know, though!

NORAH: What redhead?

EDDIE: The red-haired nurse. She had a good view. I was lying on my stomach at the time.

NORAH: While the nurse was viewing your private parts?

EDDIE: Well, not all of them. I don't think!

NORAH: Wait a minute! Why were you lying on your stomach when the doctor was doing the test?

EDDIE: I suppose, he could have done it the other way, but that might have been over-exposure.

NORAH: Let me ask you something...personal!

EDDIE: Shoot!

NORAH: Were you getting a clipping? You know, so you won't have children.

EDDIE: You mean a vasectomy? Yeah! That's it! I don't want to be a danger to the women in my dreams anymore.

NORAH: You're crazy! Now, tell me the truth. What was the doctor testing for?

EDDIE: It was nothing, really!

NORAH: Hey! I happen to like you...!

EDDIE: And, I like you..

NORAH: ...even maybe love you, if that's possible! Now, you have me worried.

EDDIE: Love me! Well, that's a nice state of affairs! We never used that word before.

NORAH: Haven't you even considered it?

EDDIE: Yes! I considered it. But, I didn't think you'd feel the same way.

NORAH: The same way?

EDDIE: Yeah! I guess I love you too! I know, I look forward to talking to you like this. I don't know what I'd do if I couldn't talk to you each night.

NORAH: That's the way I feel. I'm not sure I wanted it this way, but I'm really not disappointed. It's been a wonderful couple of months. It really has meant so much to me each night.

EDDIE: And, to me! And, I like the idea that I can say: 1 love you!

NORAH: So do I!... I love you!

EDDIE: That sounds nice...well, anyway, it spells nice!

NORAH: Nut!!!! But wait a minute, what about that test you're getting.

EDDIE: It's nothing, really! *(Forgets himself)* Just something an old guy has to watch out for!

NORAH: What's the "old guy" bit?

EDDIE: *(Tries to recover)* Did I say that? What I meant was... you know, any old guy...Look, Daphne! This is ridiculous!

NORAH: What's ridiculous? What do you mean: "any old guy."

EDDIE: Oh! You know: "any old guy."

NORAH: No! I don't know.

EDDIE: This is impossible! Here we are saying we love each other, and I'm living a lie.

NORAH: What do you mean, a lie?

EDDIE: Well, to be honest with you, I'm not a 40-year old man.

NORAH: You're not???? What do you mean....?

EDDIE: No! I'm not! And my name's not Ronnie: it's Eddie!

NORAH: Eddie! Eddie! Not Ronnie!...

EDDIE: No! I'm not Ronnie. I'm Eddie!

NORAH: And, you're not 40!

EDDIE: No! I'm not 40. In fact, I just started Social Security...

NORAH: What! You're telling me you're 65!

EDDIE: Hey! Don't go haywire on this: I'm only 62!

NORAH: Sixty two! Oh! That's so much better. Sixty two?

EDDIE: I understand that if you want to sign off right now, I'll understand but, I wish you wouldn't. Okay! I'm 23 years older than you, but we could still be friends, couldn't we?

NORAH: Friends! I just told you I love you! Friends? I'll have to think about that....62! That's something to consider!

EDDIE: I really wish you would. It means the world to me. Don't hang up!

NORAH: Believe me, I'm tempted to. I ought to.

EDDIE: Please don't! I need you to be there to talk to!

NORAH: And, I looked forward to talk to you and yes, fall in love. I won't hang up! I promise. But, I'll have to do some thinking about this relationship, if we can call it that.

EDDIE: I'd like to think it is, considering the waterfalls and the desert island and all that.

NORAH: Never mind the waterfalls!

EDDIE: But, didn't our dreams mean something.

NORAH: *(Not sure of how to handle this)* But, we were the same age then!

EDDIE: Hey! Age is just a number.

NORAH: That's what OLD people say!

EDDIE: Well, then! I'm saying it!

NORAH: Ronnie or Eddie, or whatever your name is, you certainly don't sound old.

EDDIE: I'm not, when I'm talking to you!

NORAH: Thanks for that, I think! I feel young too when talking to you.

EDDIE: But, you are young, at least younger than I am!

NORAH: *(Stumbles over words)* Oh! Yes! I am! That's right!

EDDIE: So, we're both young...you in body, me in spirit. That's not bad.

NORAH: I'll have to think about it.

EDDIE: I wish you would!

NORAH: How did we get into this age thing anyway? Oh, yes! The test!

EDDIE: Yeah! The test...

NORAH: By the way, what kind of test is the doctor doing?

EDDIE: A biopsy...!

NORAH: A biopsy?

EDDIE: Yeah! On the prostate!

NORAH: Oh! My God! Oh! Eddie!!! Eddie!!!

(SLOW BLACKOUT)

CURTAIN

End of Act One

"The Chat Room"
ACT TWO

(Norah comes onstage to answer her phone)

NORAH: Hello! Oh! Sally! ...No, I haven't heard anything for two days. I tried the chat room and got no answer...Of course, I was shocked when he told me his age... .and then when he told me about the biopsy...1 was really shocked!...It was a double-whammy! My emotions are all torn up. I didn't know what to think other than I must care for this man or else why would I act like I did?...No! He doesn't know how old I am. I didn't think he could handle my confession with all that's on his mind...Am I going to tell him? ...1 don't know. What's the use! I made such a point of being upset when he told me the truth about himself...How do I know it's the truth?... Don't do that to me, Sally! I've got to start believing something... I'm going to keep on trying to contact him. I guess I meant it when I said I love him...Yes, I know that's when we thought we were our fantasy ages...Oh, Sally! I'm so mixed up now, I don't know what to do. Okay! I'll keep in touch. *(Hangs up phone, she boots up computer)*

EDDIE: *(Enters his room .as phone rings. He answers it.)* Oh! Hello, Ted! You've been trying to get in touch with me? I'm sorry! I've been roaming the city for a couple of days. Yes, I got your calls on my machine. You were over here? When? Oh! I must have been out. No! You'd know I'd answer the bell. Look, I know you're my son and you're concerned but I've got to think this out for myself. Don't make it more than it is. I promise I'll...but I can't be maudlin either. I'm not the first to have this problem although I would like to think I'd be one of the last. Do I want you to come to the doctor's office tomorrow with me? You have to work!...Don't raise your voice already! Yes! I'd be pleased if you wanted to come with me. Pick me up at 10 in the morning. Thanks. Goodnight *(hangs up phone, picks up photo and talks to it...)*

Beatrice! Help me! Oh! I miss you terribly and I know you'd be such a help to me now. We should have grown old together. I know that after the bitterness I felt when you died, I don't deserve any help from up there. If I believe anything, I got to believe you're there. You better be…you deserve the best! I'm afraid, Beatrice, even though the worst that could happen would be that I'd stand a chance of being with you again. *(Rueful laugh)* Wonder what odds Las Vegas would give me that I'd make the "big show" and be with you? Yeah! Yeah! I know that's a bad joke. But, you used to laugh at them. You spoiled me! You made me think that all my jokes were winners! There I go, blaming you again! I'm sorry! Help me, Beatrice, please help me!

(SLOW BLACKOUT)

NORAH: *(Lights come up as Norah is sitting at the computer)* C'mon, Eddie, answer me. I'm trying to tell you that I'm sorry about my reaction when you told me about your age. And, then when I found out that you may be terribly sick, it was more than I could handle. As I think about our last conversation two nights ago, I find myself really missing you. I'll tell you, Eddie, I have to admit that even with all you've told me, I really do love you. I can't deny it even though my mind is in turmoil. Please contact me, Eddie, please! I don't want to go another day without knowing how you are. Eddie! Are you there? Okay, but I'm going to keep trying. You can count on it! *(Turns off computer and exits the room)*

EDDIE: *(enters the room, sits at computer, talks to himself)* I wonder what she's doing tonight! I just can't get up the nerve to contact her after lying the way I did and then dropping the biopsy on her like I did. It had to be too much for her. *(Looks at picture)* Does this seem silly, Beatrice? Here, I've told a woman more than 20 years younger than me that I love her. And, then I go and lie to her. I know I'll never love her as I loved you. You were special, Beatrice, and you left us far too soon. You have that part of my heart which loved every moment I was with you. But, I am lonely, Beatrice. This woman gives me some of my youth back to me. She has some of your ability to make me want to tell old jokes and kid about life. That was something I treasured in you. It was your ability to laugh and make me want to make you laugh. I so miss that! *(Turns back to computer, turns it on, starts to type)* Daphne! Are you there? I apologize for the other night. Somehow, I feel it was better to tell you how old I was even as I was telling you about my possible illness. Won't you answer me? Daphne.. .Daphne! *(Stares at computer for awhile, then turns it off)* I do want to talk to you... honest!

(BLACKOUT)

(Lights up, next morning)

EDDIE: *(On phone)* You're just starting now to pick me up! Hell, it's 10 to 10 and you were supposed to pick me up at 10 this morning. We'll never get there by 10:30. So help me, if we're late and they want to give me another biopsy because of it, I'm going to make them test you instead. See how you like it with a red-haired nurse staring at your backside. You're where? Downstairs! You were on the cell phone all the time? Oh, you think it's smart to trick a trickster! *(Hangs up)* Hell! The kid may have a sense of humor after all! *(Puts on cap and exits room)*

NORAH: *(Norah enters and sits in front of computer)* I can't keep doing this! It's frustrating to keep trying to reach him without knowing where he is. *(Boots up computer)* I'll give him one more chance!

Eddie...Eddie...are you there? Please tell me how you made out at the doctor's. *(Phone rings, she closes down computer and answers phone)*

Hello! Nothing to report! Sorry, Sally! Am I alright? To be honest, no! Look, Sally, really I'll be alright. I have to work this out myself. I understand how you want to help. You do help just by being concerned. I need that now and you've been there for me so thank you for everything. It's strange how I've been trying to visualize what he looks like. I had an image when I thought he was 40 but what does he look like at 62. I know he's not ancient, and neither am I. But, it's an adjustment which I'm trying to make and if this is going any further, he'll have to make an adjustment too. Am I going to tell him? Yes! I think I want to. I can't let this just fizzle out. If it's going to blow up, then I want to see starbursts. What will he say? Sally, I have no idea. I'd hope he'd say that he still loves me!

(SLOW BLACKOUT)

(Lights come on and Eddie is in his room on the phone)

EDDIE: Was I shocked? Look, Ted, of course I was shocked. When he told me that the biopsy showed there was some cancer on the prostate, the light at the end of the tunnel got quite close. I felt I was running out of tunnel. I know, Ted, I know! There are options and I'm thinking them over. Seeding is probably the way to go. A lot of guys my age and younger have done the radiation seeding and except for carrying around your own night light, it isn't that disturbing to your lifestyle. Hey! That's funny! As if I had a lifestyle. You think that's the approach, too? Good! We're agreed on something. No, I'm not being sarcastic, Ted! Don't get touchy at this time! I need you to listen to my old jokes. No! I don't intend to declare a moratorium on jokes. Sorry! That's final! By the way, Ted, thanks for being with me this morning. I'm sure it made your mother happy. Oh! She knows, she knows. I'll be sure to tell her! Good night! My love to the boys and Little Bea!

(Hangs up, turns to picture) We did pretty good with Ted, I'd say! *(Boots up computer as Norah enters her room, turns on computer)* Let's see if she's home and on the computer. *(Types)* Hey, there! Stranger! Are you there?

NORAH: *(Taken back)* Yes, yes! I'm here! *(Quickly, breathlessly)* Where have you been? Are you alright? Why didn't you get in touch with me? How are you? Talk to me!

EDDIE: Whoa! Give me a chance. First, I've been busy visiting the doctor and also a little shy about calling you after confessing my lie the other day.

NORAH: Are you alright!

EDDIE: Well, sorta!

NORAH: What'd the doctor say?

EDDIE: I do have cancer!

NORAH: Oh! Eddie... noooo!

EDDIE: Give me a chance to explain! It can be treated with radiation seeds. A lot of men my age and some younger have been treated this way successfully. The doctor said I caught the problem early which is good!

NORAH: Thank God!!! Tell me, you're going to be alright!

EDDIE: I can't promise forever, but the doctor seems hopeful. So does my son, Ted.

NORAH: Ted!! Your son?

EDDIE: Yes, I might as well confess to having a son, all 35 years of him...and a granddaughter and two grandsons. My God! Think of it! My son is only four years younger than you are! What the hell was I thinking?

NORAH: Don't do any thinking now about age or anything like that! Just concentrate on your health. Your granddaughter, how old is she?

EDDIE: She's four, Little Bea named for her grandmother, Beatrice, who died a little more than four years ago.

NORAH: The woman you walked up the falls with!

EDDIE: You remembered that, did you? Yes, the woman I walked up the falls with and rescued from basket sellers, and a lot of other wonderful memories. I'm sorry! I shouldn't go on like that to you.

NORAH: No! It's alright. I'm glad that you can think so wonderfully about her and that you remember happiness, especially at a time like this.

EDDIE: You're a generous woman, Daphne! I appreciate that!

NORAH: I did say I loved you...and I still do. Generosity is part of loving someone, I'd say.

EDDIE: You still love an old guy, who's old enough to be your father?

NORAH: I said...let's not talk age at this time. Yes, I still love you... and not as a daughter.

EDDIE: That sounds wonderful but it doesn't make too much sense. I'm a guy who lied to you.

NORAH: Lies are relative...a matter for the recipients of them to make a personal decision about forgiving and forgetting. I'd say I fell in love with a man, not an age bracket. And, I would say you did, too! After all, you knew that I told you I was 39. But, you made a decision to still correspond with me!

EDDIE: I guess you sounded compatible and upbeat despite what appears to be personal setbacks. Wait a minute! You're not married or anything like that, are you?

NORAH: No, I'm not married...now!

EDDIE: Then, you were!

NORAH: Yes! I helped put a guy through law school while I quit college and worked. We were married for 15 years and I was able to lead a pretty good life as a patron of the arts and a member of a country club. Then, it happened...he found a young paralegal in his office more exciting that a bored housewife and the two of them took off, at least 10 states south of here.

EDDIE: He didn't leave you destitute, did he?

NORAH: Not quite! I had to scramble to find a lawyer who wasn't a close friend of his and by the time we got to court, he had money and assets tied up 40 different ways. Since we had no children and I didn't work, the settlement and the alimony were not world-shaking.

EDDIE: In this day and age, you got shafted..I mean ...

NORA: Shafted says it all, Eddie!

EDDIE: So, what do you do now?

NORAH: I went back to college but after a couple of years, I needed to find some additional income, so I took a job working in a library, helping sort books, and doing some research.

EDDIE: But, a woman with your looks and not yet 40, there's got to be something better than that... and someone better than the guy who left you.

NORAH: Believe me, Eddie! If there are, they're few and far between. I should have suspected something when you said you were 40 and appeared humorous, comforting and sensitive all rolled up into one.

EDDIE: Those adjectives are far too generous for a guy who quit college to work for a roofing company and found his country club living playing poker at an Elks club.

NORAH: Sounds nice and normal to me, and it must have suited your wife just fine.

EDDIE: It seemed to! I made sure we had vacations and long weekends and Friday nights out to a movie or something she wanted to do.

NORAH: I believe it now when you say you're not 40.

EDDIE: I guess I accept your affirmation.

NORAH: No! Men your son's age are often too wrapped up in themselves and too often forget the courtship routine of their early years with the women they married.

EDDIE: You're probably right! I find myself reminding Ted to take time off and get away with the family. He's been better at it, now that Little Bea has come along. But, in fairness to him, his computer analysis career is demanding. His wife is a good woman and she understands and helps him. But, she makes lousy cookies...diet cookies that taste like straw.

NORAH: Maybe she thinks she's helping you with your health?

EDDIE: I'm sure of it! It's not that I'm that much overweight but I hate people telling me what I have to eat.

NORAH: I'll remember that!

EDDIE: Why would you do that?

NORAH: Because I'm serious about whatever relationship we have or think we have.

EDDIE: It won't be anything for you. There's little I could offer a vibrant woman more than 20 years younger.

NORAH: Let the "vibrant" woman make that decision.

EDDIE: I'm not into decisions just now, only to get whatever treatment I can get to help me.

NORAH: That's right! Please do everything you can do to help yourself. Promise me!

EDDIE: Okay! I promise you. But, you have to promise to keep in touch with me.

NORAH: I promise! Now, get some rest and you keep in touch too! Goodnight!

(BLACKOUT)

(Next day. Norah on phone with Sally)

Yes! We promised to keep in touch with each other. No! I haven't told him my age but I'm really going to. I think I want to exchange phone numbers with him so we can talk more naturally. I know, it's opening me up to a whole host of possible problems. But, I can't help it! I'm no longer the woman pretending to be a 39-year old willowy blonde. I really don't need to be, if I read him right! Will he forgive me for lying to him? I would hope so! I'm still talking to him even though he lied to me. Yes! Yes! I know we were two people almost the same age corresponding with each other but he really didn't know that any more than I did. So, he lied first. I don't know how I arrived at that logic but it helps me make sense of this. He was supposed to make a decision today with his doctor. I'm sure he'll contact me. Okay! I'll keep you informed.

(Eddie comes into his room and takes off his jacket. He talks to the picture)

EDDIE: The doctor made the appointment, Beatrice! In two days, I'm going into the hospital and they'll start the treatment. Radiation seeding! It's supposed to shrink the cancer without surgery. That's also an alternative if this doesn't work. Help me with the brass up there, will you? I need all the help I can get. *(Turns on computer, types)*

Daphne! Are you there? I just came from the doctor. I guess I'm set to go through with the treatment.... You're not there, are you? Well, I'll keep trying. *(Turns off computer, leaves room)*

NORAH: *(Enters her room, rushes to the computer, boots it up and then types)* Eddie! Are you there? I just got back to my place and wanted to know how you made out.... You're not there, are you? Damn! Alright! I'll be back! *(Closes computer, exits room)*

(Eddie enters, answers phone)

EDDIE: Oh! Hello, doctor! Yes, I'm definitely ready for the seeding process. You confirmed the appointment at the hospital for the day after tomorrow. Okay! You want me to be prepared to stay over night after the procedure. I can do that! I'll have my son bring me and he'll probably pick me up, too! Any idea how long the recovery or whatever you call it will take. Oh! You won't know if it's really working for almost a month. Well, I can live with that. At least, I hope I will. Sorry, doctor, just black humor on my part. It helps me get through sticky situations. You understand! Good!! I'll be there at seven in the morning, if my son can wake up in time. No! No! I was just kidding. He's an early riser. He'll pick me up alright! Thanks for your call, doctor. *(Hangs up, turns to picture)* Well, that's it, Beatrice. The doctor's ready to do the job. Please put in the good word up there! I know! I know! I know you will! *(He exits the room, blackout)*

(Lights up with Norah on the phone in her apartment)

NORAH...That's right, Sally. I've made up my mind to tell Eddie the truth about me. I know it may be complicated with him going through the cancer procedure but I don't want him under a misunderstanding about me. In fact, I'd like to visit him in the hospital, if he has to stay any length of time. I don't have any information about when the procedure will take place. I haven't been able to get in touch with him but I'll keep trying. The one thing I want is his phone number so I can contact him and at least leave a message. I don't want to lose this man. I have a good feeling about him. Sally, I know that two months' time is not enough to get to know a person usually, but, this is different. At least, I've got to believe it is. Thanks! I appreciate your good wishes! *(Hangs up, and gets on computer, boots it up as Eddie comes into his room. He sits at computer, turns it on)*

NORAH: Are you there yet, Eddie? *(Eddie sees message and types)*

EDDIE: I'm here. Well, how are you, stranger?

NORAH: Stranger! Stranger! I've been trying to get touch with you for the past three days.

EDDIE: I wish I knew. I'm sorry but here we are now!

NORAH: Yes, here we are! And, how are you Eddie?

EDDIE: I report tomorrow morning to the hospital for the "seeding" procedure.

NORAH: Then, it's all set?

EDDIE: Set as it's going to be! My son is going to take me to the hospital.

NORAH: Which one?

EDDIE: Which son? I only have one…Teddy!

NORAH: NO! NO! Which hospital?

EDDIE: Oh! It's Midtown General.

NORAH: That's not too far from here!

EDDIE: And, where's "here?"

NORAH: You really want to know?

EDDIE: Yes! I want to know.

NORAH: If you really do...

EDDIE: I really do!

NORAH: Well, it's 545 Weston Street, about six blocks from the hospital.

EDDIE: If I asked real nice...would you visit me at the hospital if I'm going to be there for awhile?

NORAH: You don't have to ask real nice or any other way...just ask!

EDDIE: Will you visit me?

NORAH: Yes! But, I've got to tell you a few things first.

EDDIE: Am I going to like what you're going to tell me?

NORAH: I hope so but... well, it's a bit like your news to me...about being Eddie and not Ronnie.

EDDIE: Your name's not Daphne?

NORAH: No! It's not Daphne!

EDDIE: What's your real name?

NORAH: Norah.. .spelled N.O.R.A.H!

EDDIE: You are a woman?

NORAH: YESSSS! I'm a woman...just not as young as I told you I was.

EDDIE: OHHHHH! How much "not as young" are you?

NORAH: Well, according to what you told me...I'm about four years younger than you.

EDDIE: Four years younger! That'd make you 58...am I right?

NORAH: You didn't have to spell it out but, yes, you're right!

EDDIE: But, you're still a willowy blonde...right!

NORAH: Not really!

EDDIE: What do you mean...not really!

NORAH: I'm brunette...somewhat petite... maybe a size ten....

EDDIE: I'm flabbergasted! You mean, the 39-year old willowy blonde has just disappeared before my eyes?

NORAH: I guess so, as did the 40-year old, tall suit model you led me to believe you were.

EDDIE: Yeah! But that was....! No, I guess you're right! Hah! We were a couple of good actors for a while there, weren't we?

NORAH: Pretty good, I'd say! But, did you really want to keep performing in our "play?"

EDDIE: It was fun while it lasted.

NORAH: And, we can't have fun, knowing what we know now?

EDDIE: It'll take a lot more work.

NORAH: I'm willing to work, if you are!

EDDIE: Do you think it'd be worth it?

NORAH: It has to be...at least, the way I feel about you...it has to be!

EDDIE: You sound pretty sure of yourself.

NORAH: And, I'm trying to feel sure of you.

EDDIE: I'm still listening..

NORAH: I haven't felt like I have during the past several weeks for a long time...too long. I know I seemed to blurt out "I love you!" but I really do. If love means caring about someone and wanting to be with someone...then I guess I'm in love with you.

EDDIE: I was hoping you wanted to see me at the hospital or somewhere.

NORAH: I'm glad...because I do want to see you.

EDDIE: How will I recognize you, the size ten brunette!

NORAH: I'll wear a brown skirt and a tan blouse.

EDDIE: I'll be the old guy giving the nurses a bad time.

NORAH: You better not be fooling around with nurses when I come!

EDDIE: Why does that sound...possessive?

NORAH: Because it is!

EDDIE: You're candid, at least! I guess I'll have to do my fooling around before visiting hours.

NORAH: Then, I'll dust the nurses for fingerprints!

EDDIE: You sound like you would!

NORAH: All kidding aside! May I come tomorrow, maybe in the early evening

EDDIE: Why don't I call you? What's your number?

NORAH: Here it is! *(Types number)* You got it written down!

EDDIE: I'm doing it now! Now, I promised the doctor and my son, I'd get to sleep so I'd be ready in the morning. You're sure you're not married or anything! No more surprises, please!

NORAH: Like I told you, I was married to a lawyer but he found a young paralegal in his office more interesting about four years ago and they're cavorting in the sunshine now.

EDDIE: So, you are divorced!

NORAH: Yes, I'm divorced!

EDDIE: Comfortably?

NORAH: Let's say, he was a better lawyer than my lawyer. I'm looking forward to a boost from Social Security. My work as a book sorter at the local library keeps me going! Isn't that grand to admit!

EDDIE: Well, you're honest...about that, I presume.

NORAH: Yes, I'm honest about that! You won't be getting a rich divorcee.

EDDIE: And, I'm not a rich widower! Just comfortably!

NORAH: Well, they do say two can live as cheap as one!

EDDIE: Sure. If one doesn't eat! You know, I don't even know your last name..

NORAH: It's Phillips...my maiden name. I took it back when my ex took off. And, come to think of it, I don't know your last name. There might be more than one 62-year old Eddie in the hospital tomorrow.

EDDIE: It's Cloran...that's C-L-O-R-A-N! You can almost sing it to the same tune as Harrigan..you know H-A-R-R-I...

NORAH: I know the tune. I've been to Irish pubs in my day.

EDDIE: Oh! Now the juicy past comes out!

NORAH: Never mind the juicy past. You better get some sleep. And I better do the same if I'm going to be a devastating 58-year old size ten brunette tomorrow!

EDDIE: I have faith!

NORAH: As do I! So there! Goodnight, Eddie...I love you!

EDDIE: Goodnight, Norah! That sounds good! I love you, too! *(They both shut off computers)*

(BLACKOUT)

(Late next night. Norah is on phone)

NORAH: *(In midst of conversation)*...so you weren't disappointed with the size ten brunette?....Your son was surprised, you say? But, he's easily surprised. So don't mind him.... Okay! Actually, he seemed quite nice and didn't really act surprised... Oh! He was surprised! He didn't think the old man had it in him to get a woman to visit him?...Well, I guess your son doesn't know you very well....I don't care as long as you do!...Well, thank you Eddie. I like to think I know you. I'm so happy you didn't look all pale and wan after your surgery... The night light? What night light? Oh! You nut! No! I didn't see any glow under the sheets! Now, get some rest! Your son said that you'll be in the hospital for a couple of more days. I promise to visit you after work tomorrow. Before I hang up, tell me....were you disappointed with what you saw when I came into the room tonight? ... *(Laughs)* Now, you're kidding! No amount of anesthesia will make you see me as a 39-year old willowy blonde. Count on it! Seriously, did I measure up? ... You still love me! Well, that's wonderful because I still love the sunny smile and pleasant man lying in that bed. I don't think we'd look bad on a desert island without the other eight women. You have a confession to make...another one?... Oh! You can't swim. Then we won't. So there! That's settled. Get some rest. You have to be tired after the day's ordeal. Yes, I love you! Goodnight! *(Hangs up phone)*

(BLACKOUT)

(Lights up.)

(Norah on phone to Sally.)

NORAH: ....Yes! Eddie looked like I thought he might after he told me the truth about his age. He has a great laugh and a good sense of humor. The hospital staff really likes him. He's so good-natured. Was he surprised when he saw me? Yes! I'd say he was.. After all, how do you really describe yourself...1 gave him a dress size, hair color and little else. We had some time together. His son left the room shortly after I came. It was nice of him to give us some time alone. His son? I'd believe he was Eddie's boy! Doesn't have the ready smile but he's a young family man with all the problems of someone with a wife and three children as well as a demanding job. Eddie said that he works hard so I guess he can be more serious than his father although I think Eddie was good-natured all his life. I think he'd rather smile than scowl. What did his son say when you left? Well, he left before I did and all he said to me was: "See you soon!" Yeah! I guess that indicates acceptance of sorts. The prognosis? We didn't talk too much about his problem but I think he's going home in a few days. We'll talk more tomorrow night when I visit.

(BLACKOUT)

(Lights come up on Eddie at computer. It is three days later)

EDDIE: Norah! I thought I'd take my time telling you how much I appreciated your visits to the hospital. I know you're at work right now but I feel like talking to you. The doctor won't know the results of the radioactive surgery for a few more weeks but I'm confident and he seems to be too. I also know that I don't want to be alone any longer. I realize that this may be sudden but...will you marry me? Maybe that's why I used your e-mail rather than the phone. You can't interrupt! I'd like to think that we could share the rest of our lives together and make each other happy by just being with each other. That probably sounds ridiculous...but I'm a person of impulse and this impulse seems right! I wait for your answer! Remember I'm fragile...a negative answer could set off a mushroom cloud! *(Smiles)* Sorry! Couldn't help myself!

(He sends e-mail and turns off computer, then looks to photo)

I can't help it, Beatrice. This woman seems right. She'll never be what you were to me but that wouldn't be fair to her to expect her to be like you. She's herself and I'm happy with that and I hope she'll be happy with me. Please understand...because I'll always treasure the love we had...and still have!

(BLACKOUT)

(Lights come up with Norah on the phone)

NORAH:...That's right, Sally, he asked me to marry him...on an e-mail, an e-mail! I don't expect the man on ask me on bended knee but on an e-mail! Okay! Sally...I know I've been thinking about it. Sure, he may be shy...although, he hasn't been shy in our chat room conversations or at the hospital...What! Give him a break. Sally! I'm not really mad, just disappointed. Yes! I'll simmer down. I promise I won't do anything rash. I'll let you know. Thanks for letting me blow off steam! *(She hangs up phone and turns on computer, types an e-mail)*

Dear Mr. Cloran:

I want to alert you to the fact that someone, using your name, proposed to me in an e-mail. Can you imagine? This "mysterious" man wants me to spend the rest of our lives together. Now, can you imagine that? This "stranger" who obviously doesn't know me well enough to meet me and talk over the matter, has the temerity to suggest such a liaison in an e-mail!

I would suggest that you check with your Internet service and see if someone has been using your e-mail without your permission.

A Friend

(She sends the e-mail, closes down the computer)

(Eddie comes into his room, boots up his computer and finds his E-mail and reads it)

(To himself)

EDDIE: Nice going, Eddie, old boy! You did it this time. She's mad... I can tell it! What'll I do? ...*(Decides)*

(Picks up phone and dials.. Phone rings in Norah's apartment. She enters and picks up phone)

NORAH: Hello!

EDDIE: *(Using officious voice)* This is America On Line! I understand you've been getting indecent proposals!

NORAH: *(Smiles, plays along)* Well, I wouldn't call them indecent...

EDDIE: Oh! Well, it seems you were dissatisfied with an e-mail from a Mr. Eddie Cloran.

NORAH: Not dissatisfied. Disappointed, maybe!

EDDIE: Well, what do you want us to do about it!

NORAH: Tell him...to get with it!

EDDIE: Get with it!

NORAH: Yes! If Mr. Cloran wants to propose, he should do it in person.

EDDIE: I'm not going to tell him that in person!

NORAH: Why not?

EDDIE: I understand, he's been seeded with radium. He'd ruin my cell phone, stop my watch and set off alarm bells.

NORAH: What are you talking about?

EDDIE: With the radium seeds in him, it'll be six months at least before he's fit to be in polite company. He won't even be able to visit his granddaughter and have her sit with him, and, if his daughter-in-law happens to get pregnant in the next six months, she'll have to give him a wide berth.

NORAH: All right! Eddie, let's cut the act! What are you telling me?

EDDIE: Norah, honey! First of all, I'm sorry about the e-mail! Secondly, the doctor thinks that the seeding is going to work. It's what they do for a guy my age when the problem is in an early stage. But, the life of the radium is about six months. My regular PSA tests will determine how well I'm doing.

NORAH: Is the doctor hopeful?

EDDIE: I'd say he is...and I'm certainly hopeful. That's why I asked you to marry me...but we had better wait a good six months before getting married or we'd set off every security alarm at airports on our honeymoon.

NORAH: Honeymoon?

EDDIE: Yes! I believe in honeymoons after marriages!

NORAH: It sounds like an idea!

EDDIE: Then, will you marry me?

NORAH: Would you take a "Yes!" for an answer?

EDDIE: I would and I will!

NORAH: Oh, by the way!

EDDIE: Yes!

NORAH: How will your "seeding" affect the honeymoon, you know, the connubial part of it?

EDDIE: Let's put it this way...we won't need champagne to get a glow on!

(BLACKOUT)

END OF PLAY

Susan Ingerson and William Hickman portray Daphne/ Norah and Ronnie/ Eddie in original production of "Chat Room" at The Bridge Theatre in Whitehall.